OPPOSING
VIEWPOINTS®
SERIES

Afghanistan

Other Books of Related Interest:

Opposing Viewpoints Series

America's Global Influence

Democracy

Human Rights

Mass Media

The Middle East

The War on Terrorism

Current Controversies Series

The Middle East

War

At Issue Series

Are Efforts to Reduce Terrorism Successful?

Can Democracy Succeed in the Middle East?

Does the World Hate the United States?

The Media and Politics

U.S. Policy Toward Rogue Nations

"Congress shall make
no law . . . abridging
the freedom of speech,
or of the press."

First Amendment to the U.S. Constitution

The basic foundation of our democracy is the First Amendment guarantee of freedom of expression. The Opposing Viewpoints Series is dedicated to the concept of this basic freedom and the idea that it is more important to practice it than to enshrine it.

OPPOSING
VIEWPOINTS®
SERIES

Afghanistan

John Woodward, Book Editor

GREENHAVEN PRESS

An imprint of Thomson Gale, a part of The Thomson Corporation

THOMSON
─────✶─────
GALE

Detroit • New York • San Francisco • New Haven, Conn. • Waterville, Maine • London • Munich

Bonnie Szumski, *Publisher*
Helen Cothran, *Managing Editor*

© 2006 Thomson Gale, a part of The Thomson Corporation.

Thomson and Star logo are trademarks and Gale and Greenhaven Press are registered trademarks used herein under license.

For more information, contact:
Greenhaven Press
27500 Drake Rd.
Farmington Hills, MI 48331-3535
Or you can visit our Internet site at http://www.gale.com

LIBRARY OF CONGRESS CATALOGING-IN-PUBLICATION DATA

Afghanistan / John Woodward, book editor.
    p. cm. -- (Opposing viewpoints)
    Includes bibliographical references and index.
    ISBN 0-7377-3303-9 (hardcover lib. : alk. paper) -- ISBN 0-7377-3304-7 (pbk. : alk. paper)
    1. Afghanistan--History--2001– 2. Afghanistan--Social conditions. 3. Women--Afghanistan--Social conditions. I. Woodward, John. II. Series: Opposing viewpoints series (Unnumbered)
    DS371.4.A33 2007
    958.104'7--dc22 #69028381   2006016708

Printed in the United States of America
10 9 8 7 6 5 4 3 2 1

Contents

Why Consider Opposing Viewpoints?

"The only way in which a human being can make some approach to knowing the whole of a subject is by hearing what can be said about it by persons of every variety of opinion and studying all modes in which it can be looked at by every character of mind. No wise man ever acquired his wisdom in any mode but this."

John Stuart Mill

In our media-intensive culture it is not difficult to find differing opinions. Thousands of newspapers and magazines and dozens of radio and television talk shows resound with differing points of view. The difficulty lies in deciding which opinion to agree with and which "experts" seem the most credible. The more inundated we become with differing opinions and claims, the more essential it is to hone critical reading and thinking skills to evaluate these ideas. Opposing Viewpoints books address this problem directly by presenting stimulating debates that can be used to enhance and teach these skills. The varied opinions contained in each book examine many different aspects of a single issue. While examining these conveniently edited opposing views, readers can develop critical thinking skills such as the ability to compare and contrast authors' credibility, facts, argumentation styles, use of persuasive techniques, and other stylistic tools. In short, the Opposing Viewpoints Series is an ideal way to attain the higher-level thinking and reading skills so essential in a culture of diverse and contradictory opinions.

In addition to providing a tool for critical thinking, Opposing Viewpoints books challenge readers to question their own strongly held opinions and assumptions. Most people form their opinions on the basis of upbringing, peer pressure, and personal, cultural, or professional bias. By reading carefully balanced opposing views, readers must directly confront new ideas as well as the opinions of those with whom they disagree. This is not to simplistically argue that everyone who reads opposing views will—or should—change his or her opinion. Instead, the series enhances readers' understanding of their own views by encouraging confrontation with opposing ideas. Careful examination of others' views can lead to the readers' understanding of the logical inconsistencies in their own opinions, perspective on why they hold an opinion, and the consideration of the possibility that their opinion requires further evaluation.

Evaluating Other Opinions

To ensure that this type of examination occurs, Opposing Viewpoints books present all types of opinions. Prominent spokespeople on different sides of each issue as well as well-known professionals from many disciplines challenge the reader. An additional goal of the series is to provide a forum for other, less known, or even unpopular viewpoints. The opinion of an ordinary person who has had to make the decision to cut off life support from a terminally ill relative, for example, may be just as valuable and provide just as much insight as a medical ethicist's professional opinion. The editors have two additional purposes in including these less known views. One, the editors encourage readers to respect others' opinions—even when not enhanced by professional credibility. It is only by reading or listening to and objectively evaluating others' ideas that one can determine whether they are worthy of consideration. Two, the inclusion of such viewpoints encourages the important critical thinking skill of objectively evaluating an author's credentials and bias. This evaluation will illuminate an author's reasons for taking a particular stance on an issue and will aid in readers' evaluation of the author's ideas.

It is our hope that these books will give readers a deeper understanding of the issues debated and an appreciation of the complexity of even seemingly simple issues when good and honest people disagree. This awareness is particularly important in a democratic society such as ours in which people enter into public debate to determine the common good. Those with whom one disagrees should not be regarded as enemies but rather as people whose views deserve careful examination and may shed light on one's own.

Thomas Jefferson once said that "difference of opinion leads to inquiry, and inquiry to truth." Jefferson, a broadly educated man, argued that "if a nation expects to be ignorant and free . . . it expects what never was and never will be." As individuals and as a nation, it is imperative that we consider the opinions of others and examine them with skill and discernment. The Opposing Viewpoints Series is intended to help readers achieve this goal.

David L. Bender and Bruno Leone,
Founders

Introduction

> *"The maelstrom Afghanistan finds itself in is the result of a range of disruptive factors, including disastrous meddling by outside powers, massive flow of arms, and murderous power struggles among Afghan warlords."*
>
> —*Michael Renner,*
> *March 2002*

The 30 million citizens of Afghanistan live in one of the poorest, unhealthiest, most dangerous nations on earth. The infant mortality rate is higher than in any other nation: 163.07 deaths per 1,000 live births. The life expectancy for the average Afghan citizen is just 42.9 years. The literacy rate is only 36 percent, and the inadequate health care system must deal with a populace that faces a high risk of hepatitis A, typhoid fever, malaria, and rabies. Afghanistan's economy is in shambles. The purchasing power of the average Afghan citizen, as measured by per capita gross domestic product, is just $800, and the country's top exports—hashish and opium—are illegal almost everywhere. These desperate conditions are the result of centuries of nearly constant coups, civil wars, invasions, and occupations. Ironically, today Afghanistan is occupied by the armed forces of many nations in an attempt to undo the damage of the past.

That a landlocked country with difficult terrain, a harsh climate, and few natural resources should have been fought over so many times may seem difficult to understand, but in earlier times Afghanistan's location in South Asia made it a crossroads of global trade along the Silk Road between China and the Mediterranean. Afghanistan was conquered by Persian king Darius I around 500 B.C., by Alexander the Great in 329 B.C., and invading Islamic armies took control of the land beginning in the seventh century A.D. Genghis Khan occupied Afghanistan in the thirteenth century, and the Persian Empire occupied the area around Kandahar in 1622. In the nineteenth century, Afghanistan became the center of a struggle for regional influence between Russia and Britain. The first Afghan War between Afghanistan and Britain took place between 1838 and 1842; the second in 1878.

Incredibly, Afghanistan's situation only deteriorated further in the twentieth century. After gaining independence in 1919, Afghanistan enjoyed a period of relative stability under the monarchy founded by Emir Amanullah. But in 1979, the Soviet Union, concerned about maintaining its influence in South Asia, invaded Afghanistan and installed a puppet president, Babrak Karmai. America's response was only symbolic—a boycott of the 1980 Olympic Games in Moscow.

For the next ten years, as the Russians struggled to establish control of the country, a determined resistance movement grew. The mujahideen, or holy warriors, inspired fellow Muslims from throughout the Middle East to join their jihad, or holy war, to eject the occupation forces. During the Cold War between rival superpowers the United States and the Soviet Union, America provided covert funding and training to some of the guerrilla groups fighting the Soviets. Weary Russian forces finally abandoned Afghanistan and withdrew in 1989, leaving a power vacuum that led to civil war among competing warlords.

Finally, in 1996 an Islamist mujahideen group called the Taliban took control of the central government in Kabul. The Taliban established a strict, fundamentalist form of Islamic government that affected all parts of Afghan society. Women were required to wear the body-covering burqa and were prohibited from working or attending school. Roaming enforcers representing the Ministry for the Promotion of Virtue and

Prevention of Vice dispensed instant justice—such as cutting off the fingers of women seen wearing nail polish, or beating women who dared to venture outside without wearing a burqa. Such seemingly innocuous activities as listening to music and kite flying were banned as un-Islamic.

As the Taliban government became increasingly isolated in the world community and desperate for funds, it welcomed the support of wealthy Saudi Osama bin Laden, who established training camps for his al Qaeda terrorist organization inside Afghanistan. By the late 1990s, Afghanistan was widely seen as a failed state that openly harbored terrorists. But only after the September 11, 2001, terrorist attacks on the United States were linked to Osama bin Laden did the world turn its attention to Afghanistan. In October and November of 2001, a U.S.-led coalition used military force to help an anti-Taliban Afghan militia called The Northern Alliance oust the Taliban from power. An international security force approved by the United Nations helped to establish order in the largely lawless land, and Western nations worked together to provide financial assistance to Afghanistan and help guide it on the path to democracy.

On October 9, 2004, Hamid Karzai became the first democratically elected president of Afghanistan, and in September 2005 a representative assembly was chosen by popular vote. These hopeful signs, however, cannot overshadow the still dismal conditions facing most Afghan people. If Afghanistan is ever to become a successful, even moderately prosperous nation, it will certainly take many more years of support from the international community. Whether Afghanistan can ever rise above its troubled past is one of the issues debated in *Opposing Viewpoints: Afghanistan* in the following chapters: Has the U.S. Invasion of Afghanistan Been Beneficial? Has Life Improved for Afghan Women Since the U.S. Invasion? How Should Drug Production in Afghanistan Be Addressed? What Is the Political Climate in Afghanistan? The wide-ranging viewpoints in this anthology will help readers to better under-stand the difficult issues facing Afghanistan and gain insight into the possibilities for that struggling nation's future.

Has the U.S. Invasion of Afghanistan Been Beneficial?

Chapter Preface

Although most polls indicate that the majority of Americans are pleased that the United States removed the Taliban regime from power in Afghanistan and helped to stage presidential and assembly elections there, the invasion has always been controversial. The public was generally eager to see a response of some kind to the September 11, 2001, terrorist attacks, but not everyone agreed that military action was the right one. Determining whether or not the invasion was beneficial depends upon whether one believes it was necessary.

In his address to the nation announcing the commencement of hostilities in Afghanistan, President George W. Bush stated that the action was a direct response to the terrorists responsible for the September 11 attacks and the regime that harbored them. He said, "On my orders, the United States military has begun strikes against al Qaeda terrorist training camps and military installations of the Taliban regime in Afghanistan. These carefully targeted actions are designed to disrupt the use of Afghanistan as a terrorist base of operations and to attack the military capability of the Taliban regime." Columnist Trudy Rubin supported the president's decision, noting, "We had been attacked on our soil and Afghanistan was harboring the criminals."

Critics of the war, however, argued that a military response to terrorism was inappropriate. They asserted that it was inevitable that innocent Afghan civilians, who had had nothing to do with the terrorist attacks, would be killed in the bombings. Wrote professor Howard Zinn, "I believe two moral judgments can be made about the war in Afghanistan: The September 11 attack constitutes a crime against humanity and cannot be justified, and the bombing of Afghanistan is also a crime, which cannot be justified." Pacifists who reject the concept of a just war believed that continued dialogue, rather than violence, was the proper response to September 11. Said activist Colman McCarthy, "The [appropriate] political response to September 11 would have been to follow the U.S. government's longtime advice to Israeli and Palestinian leaders: talk to each other, negotiate, deal, compromise, stop the killing and reconcile." Other critics saw ulterior motives for the war, such as the desire to build an oil pipeline through Afghanistan to supply America with oil or simply an imperialist grab for land and other resources. "This war is about the extension of US power. It has little to do with bringing the terrorists to justice, or with vengeance," wrote peace activists Rahul Mahajan and Robert Jensen.

By the time the Taliban regime had been removed from power in November 2001, however, a solid majority of Americans agreed with the assessment of philosopher Martha Nussbaum, who said, "I think we were justified in going to war with Afghanistan given that the Taliban regime was protecting [al Qaeda]. It was retaliation for unjust aggression." The Afghan invasion has since been overshadowed by the much more controversial war in Iraq. Many vociferous critics of the Iraq war say that the Afghan campaign, which has generated far fewer American casualties and is more justifiable, compares favorably. But support for the American effort in Afghanistan was never unanimous, and the war will likely remain a subject of debate for as long as American forces are stationed there.

| *"Afghanistan is undergoing tremendous positive changes."*

The U.S. Invasion Has Benefited Afghanistan

Michael Turner

According to Michael Turner in the following viewpoint, Afghanistan has experienced positive benefits since the U.S. overthrow of the Taliban regime in 2001. Afghan girls are being educated for the first time, the people have embraced democracy, and President Hamid Karzai is successfully fighting Afghanistan's illegal drug trade. Michael Turner is a U.S. congressman representing the third district of Ohio.

As you read, consider the following questions:

1. According to Turner, how many girls are being educated in Afghanistan today?
2. What changes have occurred in girls' education in Afghanistan, according to the author?
3. As stated by Turner, why is Hamid Karzai opposed to opium production in Afghanistan?

Michael Turner, "Afghani Success Goes Overlooked," http://www.house.gov/apps/list/hearing/oh03_turner/afghani_success.html, January 28, 2005. U.S. Department of State, Washington, D.C.

Recently, I participated in a Congressional Delegation that visited Iraq, Afghanistan, Pakistan, and a number of other countries significant in the War on Terror. While news about Iraq continues to dominate the headlines and receive the bulk of U.S. resources we should not forget about the successes we've had in Afghanistan. Since the elections in October [of 2004], over 28 million Afghanis have enjoyed their first tastes of democracy. The U.S. and our allies should not lose track of this and must continue to support the fledgling Afghani democracy.

Afghanistan is undergoing tremendous positive changes. For example, we visited an all-girls school, the size of a typical Ohio high school. However, 6,000 girls went to this school, in different shifts throughout the day. By their demeanor one would think these girls were as carefree and as typical as any American high school girl. That makes it all the more remarkable considering that just a couple of years ago these girls would not have been allowed to go to school and were barely allowed to leave the home. These women will grow up and make valuable contributions to their communities and perhaps the world.

Reasons for Success

There are several reasons why Afghanistan is experiencing success since its liberation from the [fundamentalist Taliban regime] and their recent elections.

There is a sense of an Afghani people. Afghan nationalism exists. Afghans identify themselves with Afghanistan rather than with a particular religion or a sect.

Afghanistan is a free and sovereign state. Afghanistan declared its independence from Great Britain after the third Anglo-Afghan war in 1919. Afghanistan maintained its independence and resisted several invasions from the Soviet Union, until the large scale Soviet invasion in 1979. The Soviet Union then occupied Afghanistan from 1979 until 1989.

Victory in Afghanistan

In Afghanistan, we won the war in coalition with Afghans. American power and Afghan forces were both essential to this victory. The fact that the Afghans played a key role in their own liberation gave them a sense of dignity and ownership of their destiny. Afghans in the north and the south were active participants in, not passive recipients of, the actions needed to free their country from an extremist and terrorist regime.

Zalmay Khalilzad, National Interest, *Summer 2005.*

Then the Taliban, with [the al Qaeda terrorist group's] assistance took away Afghanistan's sovereignty and controlled Afghanistan from 1996–2001. Afghans I met made it clear that they do not consider themselves Arab Muslims and considered the influences of Al Qaeda and the Taliban to be outside their country. Geographically they are located next to countries including former Soviet satellites: Uzbekistan, Tajikistan, and Turkmenistan. Therefore, Afghans truly felt liberated from oppression and outsiders when the U.S. and our coalition partners helped dislodge the Taliban.

Afghanis abhor Afghani on Afghani violence. Violence in Afghanistan arises from native Afghans seeking to protect their homes and family from outside invaders or radical extremists. Violent acts in the country are perpetrated by remnants of the Taliban attempting to destroy the newly formed democratic institutions.

The people embraced democracy. Afghans embraced democracy, not just the leaders but average citizens. The election in Afghanistan [in] October [2004] was a remarkable event, with millions of Afghans standing in line to vote, even in the face of threats from al Qaeda and the Taliban.

Hamid Karzai was an established national leader, hero, and celebrity, before becoming president. Thus, as a national leader President Karzai has the ability to persuade and influence the people of Afghanistan.

Nowhere is the leadership ability of President Karzai more apparent than in Afghanistan's challenge [of] fighting the narcotics trade. Poppies, which [are] turned into opium, the raw material used in heroin, is the quickest and most profitable crop for farmers to grow. The CIA states that Afghanistan is the world's largest producer of opium and estimates it may account for up to one-third of the nation's GDP [gross domestic product].

President Karzai has called "jihad" [holy war] against the illegal crop because it is wrong for Muslims to engage in the drug industry. Foreign and Afghan officials are forecasting a drop of between 30 percent and 70 percent in [the 2005] crop. In order to sustain this drop in opium production, the U.S. must continue to support President Karzai and encourage farmers to plant other crops and engage in other industries.

Spreading Democracy

While most of the discussion remains focused on Iraq, we must not lose sight of the success coalition forces had in liberating over 28 million Afghans. The military conflicts in Afghanistan destroyed its infrastructure and the country is extremely poor and remains dependent on foreign aid. If we help them build their economy and infrastructure, we will help spread democracy in the Muslim world.

| *"Afghanistan is not a resounding success story. . . . The socio-political situation is still uncertain and the economy is in shambles."*

The U.S. Invasion Has Harmed Afghanistan

Faruq Achikzad

According to Faruq Achikzad in the following viewpoint, Afghanistan's economy is in shambles and its political outlook is uncertain. Achikzad claims that Afghanistan is run with money earned through its production of opium, giving drug warlords enormous power. The United States has failed to follow through on its promises to help reconstruct the country after it invaded it in 2001, and the security situation is deteriorating, he asserts. Faruq Achikzad, a native of Afghanistan, is a former United Nations Resident Coordinator in North Korea.

As you read, consider the following questions:

1. According to the author, what is the source of most investment money in Afghanistan?

2. Why was the Kabul-Kandahar road completed so quickly, as cited by the author?

Faruq Achikzad, "Afghanistan Is Not a Success Story," http://www.institute-for-afghan-studies.org. Reproduced by permission.

3. According to Achikzad, what is the state of Afghanistan's infrastructure?

Contrary to what the [George W.] Bush administration is portraying to the American people, Iraq is fast becoming a deep morass and Afghanistan is not a resounding success story.

I just returned from a month long visit to Afghanistan. What I observed during my stay there was quite different than what the Administration would have us believe. Three and a half years after [President Hamid Karzai's] Government was installed in Kabul, the socio-political situation is still uncertain and the economy is in shambles.

The Taliban/Al-Qaeda elements are still at large, killing innocent people, government officials and soldiers on a daily basis.[1] [Al Qaeda leader Osama] Bin Laden, [Taliban leader] Mullah Omar and other top leadership of this network are still hiding in their fur-lined foxholes, somewhere between Pakistan and Afghanistan.

A Narco State

Afghanistan, the world's largest producer of opium, has in fact become a narco state. While some prominent warlords are, on surface, being sacked and disarmed, others, energized by narco-trafficking, are fearlessly roaming around the country.

As for the economy, telecommunications and construction have attracted substantial investment. Most of the investment in the construction industry arises from the profits generated from the opium trade. Investments in other sectors of the economy are lagging behind despite government efforts to encourage them; this is due to instability and insecurity, which, together, impede the formation of the enabling environment for investment.

1. The fundamentalist Muslim Taliban regime ruled Afghanistan before the U.S. invasion in 2001. Al Qaeda is the terrorist group responsible for the 9/11/2001 attacks; its training bases are in Afghanistan.

The use of the Afghan local currency, the Afghani, is not growing rapidly in the financial sector, due to the dominance of the US Dollar in the Afghan economy. Even outside the formal financial sector, the use of Afghani was only 10–12 percent last year [2004]. This was in spite of the fact that Afghani-Dollar exchange was kept rather stable during the same period.

Slow Progress

Further evidence of slow progress in reconstruction work has been the government's preoccupation with the . . . parliamentary election, worsening of the security situation, and a persistence of drug trafficking in the country. This multitude of problems has not allowed the Karzai government to devote much attention [to] poverty reduction. In fact, the government has yet to announce its Poverty Reduction Strategy. The consequences of this inertia have been severe: the state has failed to provide safe drinking water and sanitation for the majority of the people. The condition of Afghan refugees and displaced persons in Afghanistan has been also chaotic. While some refugees have returned home, millions are still in the neighboring countries due to the lack of shelter and other factors mentioned above.

President Bush, in a speech to the graduates of the Virginia Military Institute, in April 2002, promised to launch a Marshall Plan for Afghanistan, not understanding its original goals and implications. The Marshall Plan was intended to revitalize Western Europe, which was already industrialized and integrated in the world economy before World War II. Afghanistan, on the other hand, being a poor country, is confronted with an entirely different set of circumstances.

Despite the deferential rhetoric, the U.S. Administration has not yet delivered anything bearing even the slightest resemblance to the Marshall Plan. For example, the showcase Kabul-Kandahar road of 241 miles was built at a cost of $270 million with USAID [U.S. Agency for International Development] money. This poorly constructed road is said to be one of the costliest roads ever built in the region. For political expediency, the road was completed in great haste before the presidential election in Afghanistan. USAID haphazardly engaged several companies in this project, with little oversight.

In light of all these problems, Afghanistan has quite a long way to go towards becoming an effective and accountable state. It needs, among other things, a sustainable national budget, an effective public administration, and most importantly, stability and rule of law throughout the country. Presently, government employees as well as members of the nascent armed forces are paid low salaries, which are often in arrears. This, coupled with high prices of housing and food have resulted in endemic corruption. Further, the government ministries and departmental entities have skeletal staffs, most of which are ill equipped to perform their duties.

Escalating Violence

The increasing instability in recent months, as evidenced by escalating violence which has led to the recent US offensive in eastern and southern Afghanistan, has forced the UN [United Nations] Secretary General's envoy to Afghanistan to assert, "over the last three months a negative evolution of the nation's security has been observed" . . . and "the country is confronted with an escalation of both the number and gravity of incidents. . . ."

The American administration has hailed Afghanistan as a success. With platitudes they continue to put a happy face on an extremely complex and unstable set of affairs. But the realities on the ground in Afghanistan betray the truth. Far from being a successful effort at nation-building, the current situation, with all its attendant problems, threatens to unravel what little progress has already been achieved. How, then, in good conscience can this be deemed a success?

| *"One thing is clear: [The Afghanistan] success story is not being told."*

The Media Underreport Progress in Afghanistan

Mary Matalin

Mary Matalin is a former assistant to President George W. Bush and former counselor to Vice President Richard Cheney. In the following viewpoint she argues that the media are not reporting on the great progress being made in Afghanistan since America ousted the fundamentalist Taliban regime in 2001. Infrastructure is being rebuilt, and a free press and the rule of law are both emerging, she claims. Furthermore, Matalin maintains, the first elections held in Afghanistan demonstrate that the American invasion has created the possibility of a genuine Muslim democracy.

As you read, consider the following questions:

1. According to Matalin, why are the Afghan people grateful for the American invasion of their country?
2. What is the security status of Afghanistan, in Matalin's opinion?

3. According to the author, what will be the result if the Afghanistan success story is not told?

The first free election in Afghanistan's history was a seminal event for that country and for our own. With their votes, Afghans risked their own personal security and advanced our national security: They implemented the first concrete act of President [George W.] Bush's transformative foreign-policy strategy to replace tyranny and terrorism with liberty and opportunity. To borrow a phrase, Afghans' first step for individual freedom was a giant leap for world peace.

Despite the significance of these events—their potential to transform the Islamic world—both Western and Middle Eastern media have devoted scant coverage to them. My friend [conservative radio host] Rush Limbaugh and I were both frustrated by—and curious about—this virtual news blackout, and were delighted when USAID [U.S. Agency for International Development] gave us an opportunity to join a delegation to see the progress in Afghanistan for ourselves.

At 30,000 feet, the appeal of Afghanistan to its many invaders is clear. Flying over the miles of snowcapped mountains and sweeping plateaus positioned in one of the world's most geographically strategic intersections, I thought of the ancient conquerors—Darius, Alexander, Genghis Khan—who swept across this land; of the traders who forged the Silk Road and fused European and Asian cultures; of the British and Russians whose clandestine Great Game left Afghanistan a legacy of institutional bribery; even of the American hippies who invaded in pursuit of the most meditative mountains— and (allegedly) best hashish—in the world.

Tragic Modern History

This romantic history receded rapidly with altitude. Closer to the ground, Afghanistan's tragic modern history becomes all too evident. Between the savagery of the Soviets [who ruled the nation in the 1980s] and the Taliban [Afghanistan's rulers before the U.S. invasion], and the devastating civil war, the once lush land has been reduced to a giant pile of smoky, gray rubble; as we descended into Kabul, the crystalline blue majestic aerial Afghanistan gave way to a muddy, outdated airbase secured by barbed wire, cement roadblocks, and lots of guys with big guns.

While Rush and I were trying to digest this forbidding terrain, the USAID folks looked as if they were having a family reunion. All the soldiers seemed similarly pumped. Oddly, everyone was most enthusiastic about all the mud, which covered everything and everyone. Ushering us into "hard cars," each with "shooters" riding shotgun, the locals gave us our first dose of Afghanistan reality: The revered mud was the result of a record snowfall that could reverse the ravages of a seven-year drought. It also tamped down the usual oppressive dust—dust so pervasive it produced the infamous "Kabul cough."

The unnatural dust is the upshot of decades of deforestation at the hands of would-be conquerors. It is not easy for a Western mind to comprehend the devastation that occurred in our generation. In addition to the deforestation, the Soviets and Taliban obliterated ancient cities; poisoned wells; mined, mortared, and laid waste to irrigation systems, roads, schools, and entire villages. Historic landmarks, like the Bamiyan Buddhas, were vaporized. Millions fled the country; those who remained were transported culturally to a 12th-century Islamic-extremist world.

A Grateful Country

There is a jarring incongruity between Afghans' attitude and their environment. Despite the terror that defines their recent existence, they display no signs of self-pity or despair, no sense of entitlement. We heard the same refrain everywhere we went, from old and young: "Thank you, America," and

"Please do not leave." They want to rebuild their country themselves—but need us to help them with the tools. They admire America, and understand our mutual interest in making Afghanistan a modern country to prevent terrorists from reconstituting. They also have a keen grasp of how their democratic experiment could transform the Muslim world.

It is hard not to share their confidence that they will succeed in building a modern Muslim state; physical transformation is in evidence everywhere.

Rebuilding

One of President Hamid Karzai's highest priorities was to rebuild Afghanistan's transportation infrastructure. Bombed-out roads, collapsed bridges, and blocked tunnels literally closed the country down. Afghans view the road from Kabul to Kandahar as a symbol of Afghanistan's promise: The 300-mile strip of smooth asphalt, along with hundreds of additional miles of newly regraded roads, has dramatically improved quality of life and accelerated economic growth. The roads provided the mobility needed to expedite commerce and to construct canals, sanitation projects, power-generation facilities, housing, and market places. Progress is obvious. Giant cranes and massive scaffolding hover over the bombed-out buildings. Trucks full of construction materials and farm produce speed along beside taxis—and us, in our armored humvees and bulletproof van. (We are told such transportation is necessary for our security, but the people all wave and smile at us from their curbside kiosks full of goods that were unattainable until recently.)

The infrastructure improvements are making a dent in some of the worst living conditions in the world. The scourges of mothers' dying in childbirth, infant mortality, and infectious disease are declining steadily as hundreds of health clinics and hospitals go up and millions of children receive vaccinations. The astronomical illiteracy rates, too, are being

Elections in the Middle East

For the first time, in 2005, there were elections in Iraq—and also in Palestine, Lebanon, Afghanistan, and Egypt. Saudi Arabia allowed municipal elections, and Kuwait granted women the right to vote and run for public office. But the press made precious little of these landmark occurrences.

Carol Platt Liebeau, Human Events, *January 3, 2006.*

eroded: Thousands of new schools and tens of thousands of new teachers are meeting the pent-up demand for education. Explosive enrollment has quadrupled the student population from 900,000 to 5 million, 40 percent of which is female. We saw some innovative programs, including a [First Lady] Laura Bush concept: accelerated classes for older girls left illiterate by the Taliban.

Establishing Democracy

Keeping pace with the restoration of basic services is the even more difficult process of building institutions that undergird stability and democracy, institutions that are either totally foreign to the Afghans or had been savagely purged from among them:

A credible electoral process. Every Afghan tells you a proud story of his or her first vote. A general told me how remote villages overcame logistical nightmares by transporting ballot boxes on the backs of donkeys. Karzai has skillfully managed the potentially disruptive ancient-warlord governing system, getting the local bosses to buy into the concept of running for power in the upcoming parliamentary elections, rather than killing their way in. He is filling the new government with reformers, including women.

A free press. We saw fledgling but far-reaching print, radio, and TV operations. A disproportionate number of students we met want to be journalists. We asked one girl why. She replied, "We want to tell the truth."

Rule of law. A judiciary is forming, the militias are disarming, and the Afghan National Army is growing. The weapon-demobilization program is succeeding: We saw surreal acres of heavy weaponry collected from the former warriors.

Other hallmarks of a modern state are emerging—slowly by Western standards, but Afghans apply their own realistic standards. They are motivated by what they have overcome, rather than discouraged by how much more remains to be done.

The over $8 billion in international aid has, obviously, played a significant part in Afghanistan's progress; but there are three other factors that are making it possible. The first is Karzai himself, an exemplar of Afghan courage whose father was assassinated by the Taliban. He told a story of being stranded with eleven of his tribesmen on a mountaintop, with the Taliban in pursuit. Expecting imminent death, he used his little remaining cellphone power to call the BBC [British Broadcasting Corp.] and make them air his claim that Afghanistan would never surrender. It is with this moment in mind that he goes about the monumental business of democracy-building.

The second factor is U.S. ambassador Zalmay Khalilzad, an Afghan American with decades of experience in defense and diplomacy, who knows not only his native country inside out, but the Beltway [Washington, D.C.] levers of power as well. And the third is the unsung but enormously effective PRTs— the Provisional Reconstructive Teams of troops and aid workers who go across the country doing the hands-on work of hundreds of democracy-building programs. They feel an electric pride in their work.

The Story Is Not Being Told

Security remains difficult in places—the day we were in Kandahar, soldiers under attack shot one bad guy in the neck and captured another—and that slows down reconstruction. But because President Bush has made "development" the third "D" in his national-security strategy, along with defense and diplomacy, the troops have figured out on the ground how to accelerate the stabilization of this former terrorist haven by safeguarding the developers. Their efforts have also forged a bond of trust with the Afghan people. On one of our troop visits we heard how earlier that day they had been called to Medevac vehicular-accident victims hours from base. The husband did not want to leave his injured wife, but gave his toddler son to the soldiers—an unimaginable occurrence in the pre-PRT era.

In our four days, we only scratched the surface of Afghanistan's astounding progress, but one thing is clear: This success story is not being told. The Afghans' concern—which Americans should share—is that if the story remains untold, the promise of the democracy-building policy could be undermined. Our homeland security depends on that policy; Americans need their free press to try as hard as the new Afghan free press to get the truth out.

> *"Washington has no interest in nation building and the press has no intention of reporting on policy failures that leave 24 million people without security."*

The Media Underreport Failure in Afghanistan

Mike Whitney

According to Mike Whitney in the following viewpoint, the American invasion of Afghanistan in 2001 has returned that country to a medieval state ruled by warlords. While President George W. Bush applauds the creation of an Afghan constitution and the holding of elections, the nation is on the brink of collapse. The Bush administration makes dubious claims about progress in Afghanistan, and the pro-Bush media report them as facts, Whitney contends. Mike Whitney is a journalist and frequent contributor to Counterpunch, *a liberal online political journal.*

As you read, consider the following questions:

1. According to the author, what is the security situation in Afghanistan?

Mike Whitney, "Bush's Warlord, Misogynistic Patriots—The Afghanistan Failure," *Counterpunch*, June 2, 2004. Reproduced by permission of Counterpunch, http://www.counterpunch.org.

2. What was the real reason for the invasion of Afghanistan, in Whitney's opinion?

3. According to the author, how do the new rulers of Afghanistan compare to the Taliban?

> "These two visions, one of tyranny and murder the other of liberty and life, clashed in Afghanistan. And thanks to brave US and coalition forces and to Afghan patriots, the nightmare of the [fundamentalist Taliban regime] is over. And that nation is coming to life again."
>
> —*George Bush; War College Address*

Bush can take the podium in front of a national audience and claim success in Afghanistan without a whimper of dissent from the media. The American press has decided that any adventure pursued under the banner of "the war on terror" is just dandy with them as long as American lives are not at stake. It doesn't matter if the country is already a "basket case" (as a visiting British MP [Member of Parliament] described Afghanistan [in May 2004]) just as long as the Flag-draped coffins aren't being dumped off in Dover [England] twice a week.

Actually, Afghanistan might be in worse shape than Iraq. The American intervention toppled the Taliban regime, but has left nothing to replace it. In fact the war has returned the country to a medieval state of warlords and fiefdoms; a situation that resulted in 25 years of factional fighting and civil war.

So where does Bush get the nerve to sound off about "a nation coming to life again?"

Buried on the Back Pages

Afghanistan is buried on America's back pages; another pitiable entry in The Bush Administration's log of imperial neglect. Once the Taliban were routed and attention shifted to Iraq the country receded into predictable anarchy. There was no stopgap for the ensuing chaos; no plan to assist in the

SOME RE-ASSEMBLY REQUIRED...

BLUEPRINT FOR THE FUTURE OF AFGHANISTAN

John Branch. Reproduced by permission.

transition; just platitudes and air strikes, the panacea for whatever ails you. This seems to be the SOP (standard operating procedure) for the White House czars. Washington has no interest in nation building and the press has no intention of reporting on policy failures that leave 24 million people without security.

The press dutifully steps up its coverage when some pathetic public relations gambit is being orchestrated by [presidential adviser] Karl Rove and his Madison Ave. cohorts. That was the case with the Afghanistan Constitution; the widely "ballyhooed" first step towards democracy. As it turns out, the document could have been run through the shredder for all the value it'll have on Afghan society. The "constitution" hasn't improved the appalling security situation nor has it restrained the warlords and drug traffickers from "business as usual" in the countryside.

What difference does a constitution make to the average Afghan if he can't go 5 miles outside of Kabul without being

Media Compliance

There is an obvious pattern here: before 9-11 the media did not deem Afghanistan and its myriad problems (most of which were initiated by US policies in the 80s and 90s) worth covering. After 9-11, when it was convenient for the Bush administration to highlight mass oppression and poverty as justifications for war, the media complied. Now, despite continued mass oppression and poverty, Bush and [U.S. secretary of state Condoleezza] Rice have informed us that Afghanistan has been "saved" by our military intervention and installation of "democracy" and so it no longer needs our attention. The media continue to comply with government wishes.

Sonali Kolhatkar, Common Dreams Media Center,
March 28, 2005. www.commondreams.org.

shot or robbed? He's looking for security, not some worthless decree that serves no purpose other than a talking point on the *FOX News Hour.*

Media Responsbility

Now, the country is being pushed pell-mell towards elections, a step it is clearly not ready to make. (And a step that has forced [Afghanistan's president] Hamid Karzai to conduct secret negotiations with remnants of the Taliban on a power-sharing agreement.) The intention is simply to demonstrate the "great strides" that are being made in Afghanistan to improve Bush's reelection prospects at home. It is a purely superficial development that has no effect on the deteriorating security situation. The press has wasted a fair amount of column space on these tentative elections, promoting the image of a beleaguered third-world state as a burgeoning democracy. Once again, the American media has shown itself to be a reliable partner in the promotion of dubious policy.

Afghanistan is a tragic example of American foreign policy run amok. The promises of liberation and reconstruction have only generated more suffering and death. "Operation Enduring Freedom" was nothing more than a marketing ploy designed to project American military power into the region and secure long-coveted pipeline routes. It has created a situation that is more unstable than before. A recent report from [journalist] Kim Sengupta confirms this; "The UK *Independent* has learned that an all-party group of MPs from the Foreign Affairs Committee has returned from a visit to the country shocked and alarmed by what they witnessed. They warn that urgent action must be taken to save Afghanistan from plunging further into chaos because of Western neglect."

A Cynical Misadventure

This is the reality of the Afghanistan campaign; a nation teetering towards anarchy because it fit nicely into the global designs of a handful of fanatics in Washington. It is a reality that has been scrupulously omitted from the establishment press because it doesn't exemplify the virtue of American warmongering. A faithful rendering of the facts of the Afghanistan war would convince the American people that it was a cruel and cynical misadventure that never should have taken place. Nearly, three years after the end of major hostilities, the country is still more fractured and unsettled than ever. Large swaths of the country are engaged in an unreported war and the drug trade is fueling even greater instability. The Taliban have been replaced by the equally misogynist warlords who rule with an iron fist and have a similar disregard for basic human rights.

This state of affairs won't be reversed by America's paltry commitment of troops and resources, nor will it be improved by saccharine stories of Afghan elections and constitutions. Afghanistan is on the brink; driven by (to use George Bush's words) "a totalitarian political ideology pursued with consuming zeal and without conscience." This ideology was the real impetus for our war in Afghanistan.

It's doubtful that either Bush or his friends in the media will be able to keep Afghanistan out of the headlines much longer. This mess bears the American imprimatur, and sooner or later those chickens will be coming home to roost.

> "*The successful election is . . . a signifi-cant step toward victory in the civilized world's global war on terrorism.*"

Afghanistan's Elections Were a Benefit of the U.S. Invasion

Austin Bay

According to Austin Bay in the following viewpoint, the 2004 presidential election in Afghanistan was an important victory in the global war on terror. Despite attempts by former Taliban rul-ers to disrupt the election, Afghans turned out to vote in large numbers. Bay contends that electoral success in Afghanistan proves that America's plan to combat terrorism through the spread of democracy is working. Austin Bay is a nationally syn-dicated columnist.

As you read, consider the following questions:

1. According to the author, why did the 2004 presidential election in Afghanistan not receive much attention in the media?

2. What were the primary obstacles to a successful election in Afghanistan, according to Bay?

3. In the author's opinion, for what regions of the world should Afghanistan be a model?

In the age of the Internet and global communications, there are times that history-shaping news still moves at the pace of a human step or a donkey trot.

Trickling out of Afghanistan—at a rate far too slow for cable television's instant experts—is news of October's most important election: the presidential vote in Afghanistan. The election took place Oct. 9 [2004], but it took two weeks to count the votes. Ballot boxes from rural areas had to be carried by men and pack animals to central counting sites. The time lag frustrated the Western media's shortsighted demand for the quick gratification of headline success or failure.

A Significant Election

Despite the spotty international media coverage, Afghanistan's election is extraordinarily significant news. It is significant for the people of Afghanistan. It is significant for the forgotten, trampled, robbed, and oppressed people suffering in Earth's various Third World tyrannies and hard corners—those who do long for freedom's fairer shake.

The successful election is also a significant step toward victory in the civilized world's global war on terrorism. This war is as much a war against fear, poverty, and anarchy as it is a war against the petty tyrants who harbor and sustain terrorists. The 8 million Afghans who rejected fear and voted, despite threats from al Qaeda [terrorist group] and Taliban [ousted fundamentalist regime] holdouts.

Rejecting Terrorism

Rejecting fear is a defeat for terrorism. An international poll watcher reported that when the Taliban blew up a bridge north of one polling place, the Afghan voters forded the stream and kept coming. At Polling Center 217, the same poll watcher

Robert Ariail. Reproduced by permission.

found a "veritable parade" of women in blue burkas waiting to vote (yes, in a predominantly Muslim country with no history of democracy, men and women voted). The Afghan people acted, ignoring death threats made by religious fascists, the destruction wrought by 30 years of war and the lack of "a modern transportation and communication infrastructure" (i.e., roads and telephones).

The Afghan people understand [that] democracy and the rule of law are the keys to modernity as well as the foundations of a more just society, and they made a public statement about their own hopes for the future. It's a future where the governed have a legal voice. It's a future where the rule of law replaces the whim of the tyrant.

Bullets, Money, and Ballots

The Afghan vote exemplifies the ballot component of the U.S. global strategy of bullets, money, and ballots. The bullets are combat and security operations. The money is financial, reconstruction, and developmental aid. The ballot is shorthand for fostering consensus-based governmental institutions and reinforcing the rule of law.

American voters take note. Ten million Afghans registered to vote; 8 million voting translates into a whopping 80 percent turnout in a nation where land mines and the Himalayas are real voting hazards. American voters moan about the hassle of waiting in line to cast a ballot.

A Shout for Freedom

Let the nuanced critics of elections and the usual naysayers who denigrate the global appeal of democracy bicker over details. Certainly ballot security in Afghanistan is a legitimate issue, but the big picture is a loud shout for freedom. The Afghan people, in astounding numbers, went to the polls when they were given the opportunity—the first time in history they had the chance.

With 96 percent of the votes tabulated, Afghanistan's Joint Electoral Management Body named President Hamid Karzai as the likely winner [Karzai was the official winner]. Mr. Karzai received 55 percent of the vote (4.2 million votes). Former Education and Interior Minister Yunus Qanuni placed second with 16 percent (1.2 million votes).

A candidate must receive at least 50 percent plus one of the votes in order to be elected president. This is a requirement designed to limit the power of splinter ethnic, religious and militant factions. Electoral success in the geographically and ethnically divided nation thus requires cooperation and compromise. Over the next few years, several analysts see two "big tent" parties forming in Afghanistan: a secular party of some type and a moderate Islamic party.

If this sounds like a model for the rest of Central Asia and the Muslim Middle East—guess what, it is.

> *"This electoral charade will no doubt . . . be triumphantly hailed by the Bush administration as a vindication of its criminal policies."*

Afghanistan's Elections Were a Sham

Peter Symonds

According to Peter Symonds in the following viewpoint, the Bush administration used the 2004 Afghan election to deflect attention away from problems in Iraq, which the United States invaded in 2003. Bush claims that the Afghan election demonstrates that his policy of fighting terrorism by spreading democracy has been successful. The election, however, has been plagued by intimidation and corruption, primarily from U.S.-backed warlords, Symonds contends. He also claims that Afghan president Hamid Karzai is an American-controlled puppet and that the entire election was staged to aid President Bush in his own reelection bid. Peter Symonds is a member of the editorial board of the World Socialist Web Site.

As you read, consider the following questions:

1. According to the author, what influence do warlords exert in Afghanistan?

Peter Symonds, "Afghanistan's Presidential Election: A Mockery of Democracy," World Socialist Web Site, October 2, 2004. Reproduced by permission.

2. How did the United States control the Afghan election, according to Symonds?

3. As stated by the author, what groups pose the greatest threat of violence to Afghan voters?

Confronting a deepening disaster in Iraq, US President [George W.] Bush has attempted to deflect public attention by pointing to Afghanistan and its presidential poll on October 9 [2004] as a beacon of light. Bush's loyal ally in Australia, [prime minister] John Howard, who is up for reelection on the same day, has also hailed the Afghanistan ballot as a success story, demonstrating that the US-led intervention has brought "democracy" to the country.

These empty claims do not, however, bear scrutiny. Every aspect of the election has been marred by bribery, threats and thuggery—not so much by supporters of the ousted Taliban regime, but by US-backed warlords, tribal leaders and militia commanders who have been part of the current Kabul administration, and, in some cases, are presidential candidates. To describe the . . . Afghan poll as "democratic" is simply a sham.

Warlords and Their Militia

The US-based Human Rights Watch (HRW) issued a report [in October 2004] detailing the extensive abuse of democratic rights by warlords and their militia in virtually every area of the country. Based on months of research in Afghanistan, it outlines the systematic intimidation of political rivals, journalists, election organizers and the coercive methods used to ensure the support of ordinary voters. . . .

Gangsters

In the eastern areas, for instance, two militia commanders, Hazrat Ali and Haji Zahir, dominate every aspect of life. It is an open secret that these gangsters are involved in a variety of criminal enterprises and abuses, including the seizure of land, theft, kidnapping and extortion. Yet Haji Zahir is allied to current President Hamid Karzai, and Hazrat Ali operates closely with US military forces. Both are now engaged in voter intimidation. . . .

The situation is similar in the northern region around Mazar-e-Sharif, which is dominated by three militia commanders: the Uzbek warlord General Rashid Dostum; an ethnic Hazara faction led by Mohammad Mohaqqiq and the Tajik militia led by Atta Mohammad. The first two are among the 17 candidates challenging Karzai for the presidency. Atta Mohammad is allied to Jamiat-e-Islami, the Northern Alliance faction, which is backing Yunis Qanooni, widely regarded as Karzai's chief rival.

[In October 2004], Dostum held one of the few public rallies of the campaign. Some 30,000 supporters were herded into a stadium in the northern town of Shiberghan to hear the candidate absurdly promise, among other things, to defend democratic rights. Dostum is notorious throughout the country for his many atrocities, including the slaughter of hundreds of unarmed Taliban prisoners in the immediate aftermath of the Taliban regime's collapse in 2001. Until he declared his presidential candidacy, he was Karzai's top security adviser.

Voter Intimidation

The US-backed Karzai, an ethnic Pashtun from southern Afghanistan, relies on similar methods. While in these areas political parties and candidates have to contend with armed anti-US insurgents, the main threat still comes from local militia. "Numerous and separate sources in Kandahar, including political organisers, journalists and UN [United Nations] and Afghan human rights monitors, told Human Rights Watch in August [2004] that local commanders and leaders have intimidated or threatened political organisers who do not support Karzai's candidacy," the HRW report stated. . . .

American Coercion

In many ways, however, the thuggery of the warlords and tribal elders are dwarfed by the scope of the methods used by a far more powerful gangster—the Bush administration. Like these petty local despots, the US does not hesitate to use its military force and effective control over the government's purse strings to call the shots on a broader case throughout Afghanistan as a whole.

The US administration, with the assistance of the UN and the acquiescence of its European allies, has had a major hand in every aspect of the election—from its timing to the drawing up of the Afghan constitution. The Afghan people have had no say in the process whatsoever.

Two elections—for the presidency and the parliament— were due to take place in June, but were twice delayed. Now only the presidential poll will take place on October 9—carefully timed to maximise the benefits for Bush in his own presidential campaign. Significantly, Karzai has rejected calls for a further delay by many of his rivals who have cited the short period of official campaigning and a lack of security as serious impediments to open political debate.

The delay of parliamentary elections until April [2005] is even more ominous. Under the constitution, drawn up under the supervision of US and UN officials and rubberstamped by a stage-managed *loya jirga* [tribal assembly], the president has extensive autocratic powers: to appoint and sack the cabinet, military officers, judges, diplomats and other top officials. Parliament provides the only limited check on the president, but it will not be in place for six months—at the very least.

Washington's Man

Despite its formal profession of neutrality, there is no doubt whatsoever that Washington favors the incumbent. Karzai was installed with US backing in 2002 and [since then] has demonstrated his complete subservience to his American masters.

Imposing Order

In reality the Afghan presidential elections will be a test not of "Afghan democracy," but of Bush's ability to impose his political order on a country. An editorial in *Newsday* holds that, "Historic elections in Afghanistan and Iraq are key goals of U.S. foreign policy, especially for President George W. Bush, who is campaigning on his determination that they be held on schedule."

Jim Ingalls and Sonali Kolhatkar, CommonDreams.org,
October 7, 2004. www.commondreams.org.

A private US security firm, Dyncorp, provides his bodyguards, and he is ferried around the country by the US military—privileges that none of his rivals enjoy.

An article published . . . in the *Los Angeles Times* makes clear that the US is actively seeking to manipulate the election process. One of the presidential candidates Mohammed Mohaqqiq told the newspaper that US ambassador Zalmay Khalilzad had visited his office and, in the course of an hour-long discussion, attempted to talk him into withdrawing his candidacy. "He told me to drop out of the elections, but not in a way to put pressure. It was like a request," Mohaqqiq said. . . .

A Staged Election

It was not an isolated incident. "It is not only me," Mohaqqiq explained. "They have been doing the same thing with all candidates. That is why all people think that not only Khalilzad is like this, but the whole US government is the same. They all want Karzai—and this election is just a show."

Khalilzad has, of course, denied any interference in the election. But Mohaqqiq's remarks were supported by other candidates, who held a meeting . . . to discuss the issue. Sadat

Ophyani, campaign manager for Yunis Qanooni, told the newspaper: "Our hearts have been broken because we thought we could have beaten Mr Karzai if this had been a true election. But it is not. Mr Khalilzad is putting a lot of pressure on us and does not allow us to fight a good election campaign."

American Control

The note of resignation in Ophyani's comments reflects the fact that all of the country's powerbrokers, militia commanders and tribal chiefs operate under US overlordship—as they are all well aware. Their government positions and titles, the flow of financial aid to their regions and the continued existence of their militia are all dependent on the support—formally of Karzai, but in reality of the US. Ever since the fall of the Taliban in 2001, Khalilzad has been Washington's man on the spot—first as Bush's special envoy, now as US ambassador—manipulating the political situation and ensuring the local warlords toe the line.

In mid-September [2004], amid factional fighting in the western city of Herat, Karzai stepped in to dismiss Ismail Khan as provincial governor. The snap decision provoked an angry reaction from Khan's supporters who mounted a demonstration outside the UN compound in the city. The protest was forcibly dispersed by US and Afghan troops, who killed at least seven of Khan's supporters and wounded 20. While Karzai issued the dismissal, there was no doubt who was pulling the strings. As rioting threatened to get out of control, Khan—at Khalilzad's urging—appeared on local television to calm the protesters.

Pointing to Khan's removal, Khalilzad bragged ... that Afghanistan had "broken the back" of the warlords. In fact, the dismissal of Khan as provincial governor has done little to undermine his power and influence within Herat. He still retains one of the country's largest militias and has accumulated substantial financial resources through his control of the sizeable cross-border trade with neighbouring Iran. As Khalilzad is well aware, the US cannot afford to dispense with warlords like Khan, on which it has relied [since 2001]. The dismissal of Khan as governor did, however, provide a timely reminder to all of the country's despots that they hold their fiefdoms under US sufferance.

The result of the October 9 election [Karzai was declared the winner] appears to be a foregone conclusion. But even in the unlikely event that Karzai is forced to a second round and is defeated, his successor will have no choice but to do Washington's bidding. Whatever the outcome, it will certainly not be an expression of the free will of the Afghan people. Yet this electoral charade will no doubt receive the blessing of the United Nations and be triumphantly hailed by the Bush administration as a vindication of its criminal policies.

Periodical Bibliography

The following articles have been selected to supplement the diverse views presented in this chapter.

Joel Brinkley, Ruhullah Khapalwak	"Rice, Visiting Violent Afghanistan, Still Finds Political Progress," *New York Times*, October 13, 2005.
Carlotta Gall	"Taliban Battle Afghan Forces in Drug Region," *New York Times*, February 4, 2006.
Economist	"Where's the Justice? War Criminals Hold Positions in Government, Parliament," January 21, 2006.
Frederick W. Kagan	"Did We Fail in Afghanistan?" *Commentary*, March 2003.
Zalmay Khalilzad	"How to Nation-Build: Ten Lessons from Afghanistan," *National Interest*, Summer 2005.
Nicholas D. Kristof	"A Scary Afghan Road," *New York Times*, November 15, 2003.
Tim McGirk, Khakrez Muhib Habibi	"War in the Shadows: Four Years After the Ouster of the Taliban, the Fighting in Afghanistan Is Growing Deadlier," *Time*, October 10, 2005.
National Review	"The News from Afghanistan Is Good, Which Is Why the Media Have Gone Quiet on It," *National Review*, December 31, 2005.
Ahmed Rashid	"Friends of the Taliban," *Far Eastern Economic Review*, September 11, 2003.
Radek Sikorski	"Meanwhile, in Afghanistan, How It's Going, Three Years After Invasion/Liberation," *National Review*, October 11, 2004.
S. Frederick Starr	"A Sweet Sixteen: Plenty of Reasons to Cheer the Post-Taliban Afghanistan," *National Review*, August 11, 2003.
Sami Yousafzai and Ron Moreau	"Unholy Allies; The Taliban Haven't Quit, and Some Are Getting Help and Inspiration from Iraq," *Newsweek*, September 26, 2005.

CHAPTER 2

Has Life Improved for Afghan Women Since the U.S. Invasion?

Chapter Preface

Before the terrorist attacks of September 11, 2001, most Americans paid little attention to the Muslim world. That all changed after the attacks, when America responded by invading Afghanistan, a Muslim nation whose hard–line fundamentalist Taliban leadership harbored the terrorists responsible for the attacks. Many Americans were shocked at images of what they perceived to be the widespread mistreatment of women in Afghanistan by Taliban regime. The most powerful symbol of this mistreatment was the burqa, a loose-fitting garment that covers a woman's body from head to toe, with only a small mesh screen over the eyes to allow the wearer to see. American conservatives and liberals alike expressed their revulsion toward the burqa. The Feminist Majority Campaign's Norma Gattsek called the burqa a "symbol of the total oppression of women." Conservative columnist David Frum wrote that the burqa covers a woman "as if she were something so disgusting that no eye could bear to see her." In fact, however, veiling is intended to protect women from sexual predation.

Covering or veiling for modesty is a common practice in the Islamic world, and the burqa is simply the most extreme style of veiling. Many Muslim women wear the less restrictive hijab, which consists of scarves that cover the hair, neck, and sometimes shoulders. Iranian women generally wear the chador, a full-body cloak that does not necessarily cover the face. The nikab, which is worn by the Muslim women of Morocco, is a true veil that covers the face from the bridge of the nose to the chin.

Although the burqa may be unique to Islam, the practice of veiling in itself is not. Some examples of women wearing veils or head coverings in the West include brides, nuns, and widows. Traditional Hindu women also wear veils. The practice of veiling existed many years before the advent of Islam.

In fact, it was only after two centuries that the veil became common in Muslim nations, and it was not universal until about the tenth century. But in the twentieth century, the burqa has become recognized everywhere as a symbol of the more repressive fundamentalist strain of Islam and has been attacked by those attempting to build secular Islamic states. The founder of the modern state of Turkey, Mustafa Kemal Ataturk, was highly critical of the veil as he attempted to build a wall separating mosque and state. Reza Shah Pahlavi banned the veil when he first came to power in then-secular Iran in the 1930s. When fundamentalists overthrew the shah in the 1970s, one of the first acts of the new theocratic regime was to reinstate mandatory veiling.

After the fall of the Taliban in Afghanistan, most Americans expected the newly liberated Afghan women to discard their burqas. Some did replace their burqas with the hijab or a simple headscarf, but many chose to continue wearing their burqas, which caused great surprise and consternation in the West. The wearing of the burqa may well be an indicator of a lack of freedom for women in Afghanistan, but Afghan women believe there are other, more important indicators, such as the degree to which they are allowed to participate in business, government, and education. In assessing whether life has improved for Afghan woman since the U.S. invasion, many analysts continue to monitor how many women continue to wear the burqa.

> *"Significant developments favoring the growth of women's empowerment and gender equality in [Afghanistan] have taken place."*

Afghanistan Is Working Toward Gender Equality

Masooda Jalal

According to Masooda Jalal in the following viewpoint, originally given as a speech at the 49th session of the United Nations Commission on the Status of Women in March 2005, Afghan women are now escaping from the miserable oppression of the Taliban, which ruled Afghanistan before the 2001 U.S. invasion. Although Afghan women's health care, education, and legal protection is still limited, she notes, the newly elected government has taken steps to empower women and will continue to work toward full equality. Women are now assured political participation, and the government is actively eradicating customs that harm women, Jalal asserts. Masooda Jalal is the Minister of Women's Affairs in the Islamic Republic of Afghanistan.

Masooda Jalal, "Remarks at the 49th session of the UN Commission of the Status of Women, March 2005," www.un.org/webcast/csw2005/statements/050302afghanistan–e. pdf, March 2005. Reproduced by permission.

As you read, consider the following questions:

1. According to Jalal, what was the longer range impact of the Taliban's treatment of Afghan women?

2. What was the significance of the participation of women in the drafting of the Afghan constitution, according to the author?

3. As cited by Jalal, what are some significant achievements of the Ministry of Women's Affairs in Afghanistan?

This is a historical moment for the women of Afghanistan, as it is the first occasion in which we are officially represented in a global meeting on women. We missed the first four world conferences on women, as well as the Beijing plus Five [a UN conference on women held in Beijing in 2000]. However, today, we are in your company. This is because we now have a government and political environment that permits Afghan women to be heard, represented, and to create a path where they could lead and be productive in the service of our country and people.

A Glimpse at Our Women's Situation

The story of our women is one that is inextricably linked to the story of our nation. The world watched with awe and interest as a new wave of optimism unfolded following the collapse of the Taliban rule three years ago [in 2001]. It was like coming out from the dark after 23 years of quiet solitude. We also acknowledge that the shackles we carried during the past 23 years may have been broken, but continue to stand in the way of our vision.

War destroyed the foundations necessary for the growth and progress of Afghanistan as a nation. Due to a lack of statistical capacity, as a result of those twenty-three years, we cannot describe with accuracy the extent in which women suffered in Afghanistan. Our story is a living example of the worst that could happen to women under the regime of despotism, lawlessness and armed conflict.

Nevertheless, we have been taking positive steps since [2001]. With the help of the international community, we put together some data that provides a clearer picture of where we stand in our efforts to advance the status of women. Data reveals that there are many issues that afflict the lives of our women. However, the worst indicators could be found in the areas of health, education, economy, legal protection of human rights and political participation.

Health and Population

Women represent 48.6 percent of an estimated 22.2 million people in Afghanistan. While women in developed countries generally live longer than men, life expectancy of women in Afghanistan is forty-four [years], one year shorter than their male counterparts. Maternal mortality rate is 1,600 per 100,000 live births, believed to be second highest in the world. The infant mortality rate is 115 per 1,000, while fertility rate is placed at 6.8.

[In 2004], health expenditure (per capita) amounted to only US$1, in contrast to the average US$21.0 among countries of South Asia. Almost half of the deaths among Afghan women—within the reproductive group—result from complications of pregnancy and childbirth. Twenty-three years of exposure to violence, conflict and *public execution rituals* have left many Afghan women psychologically traumatized and in dire need of therapeutic assistance. Forced marriages—occurring mainly during puberty—inadequate reproductive health services and facilities, poverty, lack of female health practitioners, unfavorable traditional beliefs and practices, and many other factors have prevented our women [from achieving] proper health conditions.

Education

The Taliban [fundamentalist Islamic rulers of Afghanistan from 1996–2001] imposed repressive edicts that severely stunted the learning and thinking capacities of our women. In the region of South Asia, the women of Afghanistan have the lowest literacy rate (10 percent). Over 1 million girls, between the ages of 7–13, remain out of school. The completion rate of primary education for females is 0.4, while men rate at 15.0. In addition, based on the total figure, the average years of schooling is 0.8 for females and 2.6 for males. Distance between schools and communities, lack of transportation, restriction on girls' mobility, poverty, lack of interest in education, shortage of female teachers and schooling for girls, male preference, coupled with a lack of security, and poor instructional materials are among the challenges faced by women in the field of education.

Economic

Despite recent progress in the field of economy, approximately 70 percent of the country's population continue to live in extreme poverty, with women experiencing the worst consequences. Women predominantly work in the informal sector (agriculture, commerce, manufacturing, handicraft, and transport), which accounts for 80–90 percent of the total economy. Economic projects are available, but few, palliative, unsustainable and too micro to create meaningful impacts. Women's economic potentials are hampered by a lack of education, restricted mobility, inadequate capital and technical services, lack of access to markets, low productive capacity, lack of infrastructures for product transport and storage, as well as poor technology. In addition, the contribution of women to the economy has been undervalued, while they continue to not have control over their income.

Legal Protection

Legal protection for all should exist within the framework of national laws. However, due to a lack of knowledge of their rights and a culture that generally supports the subordination of women; the majority of women are deprived of equal protection before the law.

A wide range of acts of violence against women and girls are reportedly committed in the name of religion and tradition. Domestic violence, early marriage, forced marriage, and a practice of marrying off women to settle disputes continues to remain rampant. In the most desperate of situations, women either threaten to, or actually [do], commit self-immolation. The rights of women are ignored within the family, while the closest external source to mitigate the problem remains the village Shuras (a village justice mechanism). Whereas, some of the Shuras have started to include women as members, lack of gender sensitivity has rendered women helpless in the face of injustice. Moreover, family and community frown upon women who present their case outside the home.

Politics and Public Life

Participation of women in public life remains extremely low. Their representation in the civil service and in international development agencies also remains insignificant. Their consciousness of public issues is poor, while the general belief that women's activities should be restricted [to] domestic spheres continues to exist. There are NGO's [nongovernmental organizations] that are working actively to promote gender awareness and women's rights. However, they lack capacity and resources. They need support.

Steps that We Have Taken

In spite of all the challenges, significant developments favoring the growth of women's empowerment and gender equality in my country have taken place. On December 14, 2003, the Constitutional Loya Jirga [tribal assembly] convened with the unprecedented participation of 102 women of the 502 delegates. As such, women comprised 20% of all delegates. Afghanistan's new constitution was promulgated in January 2004 with explicit provisions concerning non-discrimination, equality between men and women, and protection of women in various sectors such as education and health. Moreover, the Constitution also ensures the right of women to political participation. In this context, the Government has been mandated to take appropriate measures aimed at preventing and eradicating negative customs contrary to Islam.

In addition, the Government has ratified and acceded to the Convention on the Elimination of All Forms of Discrimination Against Women (CEDAW), and with the assistance of UNIFEM [United Nations Development Fund for Women] is currently working with a technical assistance mission from the Division for the Advancement of Women (DAW) to enhance our capacity in fulfilling our State obligations at the highest levels.

We have a Ministry of Women's Affairs, of which, I have the privilege of serving as current Minister. Our mandate is to facilitate gender mainstreaming and provide policy advice to the Government. [Since 2001], we have been able to secure allocations from the National Development Budget. We have also established supportive mechanisms such as an inter-ministerial working group to mainstream gender in statistics, as well as an NGO coordinating Council consisting of the four largest NGO coordinating bodies in the country. This body will help monitor the achievements of its members in regard to women, and will also function as a consultative and advocacy mechanism to support our work on gender mainstreaming.

We have signed a memorandum of understanding with 11 ministries to build capacity for gender mainstreaming at the ministry levels. Training has been conducted for key officials of five ministries, including provincial partners. Additional training programs will be completed [in 2005]. In this regard, a gender training institute, in partnership with Kabul University, is expected to be inaugurated to institutionalize formal gender courses for Government staff and their partners.

Ministries have also taken steps to advance the status of women. The Government of Afghanistan has created an inter-ministerial Committee on the Eradication of Violence against Women and signed a protocol with them on specific measures to prevent and eliminate violence against women. Curricula and learning materials are being reviewed for gender sensitivity. Policies have been adopted to facilitate the securing of business licenses, particularly for women entrepreneurs. Computer and English training courses have been provided to women in Government, including kindergarten and day care facilities for their children.

The international community has played an important role towards the empowerment of women in Afghanistan, as contained in the Report of the Secretary General. I am taking this opportunity to express the heartfelt appreciation of my Government for the support rendered in helping us rebuild our nation.

We Will Keep Moving On

Despite progress achieved, much remains to be accomplished. We are aware of our objectives and want to be strategic in accomplishing them. Nevertheless, we need your support. Upon conclusion of this meeting, we will report to our Government the highlights of this meeting and begin work on formalizing a national plan of action within the framework of the 12 areas of concern, as contained in the Beijing Platform for Action. This will serve as a reference point for the planning, budgeting, monitoring and reporting of the Government on implementing measures towards the advancement of women.

We also want to assess the manner in which development assistance is being utilized in Afghanistan. We are seeking to adopt a policy that will allocate a certain percentage of project funds for mainstreaming gender, ensuring that women benefit from development projects on an equal basis with men.

Given the forthcoming [2005] Parliamentary elections, we are currently engaged in dialogue with political parties, so as to ensure the inclusion of women in their party tickets as well as the inclusion of women's agenda in their party platforms. We are also working with the Independent Administrative Reform and Civil Service Commission to guarantee equal competition between women and men, under an affirmative action policy, during the recruitment of new staff under the Priority Reform and Restructuring Program of the Government. In the meantime, we are trying to build a network of women, already members of the Government, to create a constituency support-base within the ministries.

Committed to Improving the Lives of Women

In conclusion, I would like to extend, on behalf of my delegation, gratitude and congratulations to the Commission on the Status of Women for having convened this very important meeting. We trust that this meeting will pay attention, not only to the needs and concerns that are common to many countries, but also to those that may be unique in a country like Afghanistan, that are equally pressing and important in redeeming women's dignity and freedom. Among others, we need a strong women's health program, including reproductive and mental health.

The Government of Afghanistan reiterates its commitment to achieving the Development Millennium Goals, in particular the empowerment of women and achieving gender equality. We are also in need of strategies that will enable our women to run for elections and perform with a vision of gender equality. We need to build an alliance with all of you in order to learn from your past experiences and to share with you our experience in rising from the ashes of war. We need more girl's schools and female teachers, as well as sustainable economic opportunities for our women.

I began by saying that our story was a living example of the worst that women could experience under a regime of despotism, lawlessness and armed conflict. Let me finish by saying that we want our country to be an example of how best women can rise from extreme oppression with the assistance of the international community. To all of you who refuse to tire in the process of helping the women of the world: Thank you very much, and we remain with you in this noble undertaking.

> "The situation of women in Afghanistan remains appalling."

Afghanistan Is Not Working Toward Gender Equality

Nazir Gul

According to Nazir Gul in the following viewpoint, the new government of Afghanistan has proven itself unwilling or unable to protect the rights of women. Afghan women are afraid to go out in public, where they are often abused or raped, Gul claims. Women are also afraid to attend school, contends Gul, after several girls' schools were torched. According to Gul, a bill of rights for Afghan women is urgently needed. Nazir Gul is a human rights activist and former United Nations official in Kabul, Afghanistan.

As you read, consider the following questions:

1. According to Gul, why are Afghan women still at risk of sexual violence?
2. Is the Karzai government promoting equality for women, according to the author?
3. In the author's opinion, what steps must the government take to improve the status of women in Afghanistan?

Nazir Gul, "Women in Afghanistan: Rhetoric vs. Reality," *Green Left Weekly*, May 5, 2004. Reproduced by permission of Green Left Weekly, http://www.greenleft.org.au.

The rights and status of women in Afghanistan became an issue of global concern before the military intervention by a US-led coalition that led to the end of the [fundamentalist Muslim] Taliban regime in November 2001.

The international community, including members of the coalition, made repeated undertakings that their intervention would support women in realising their rights. Colin Powell, US secretary of state, declared: "The recovery of Afghanistan must entail the restoration of the rights of Afghan women. And the rights of the women of Afghanistan will not be negotiable."

Taliban Rule

During the rule of the Taliban, the United Nations [UN], Amnesty International and other human rights organisations repeatedly highlighted serious concerns regarding the situation of women in Afghanistan. The rigid social, moral and behavioural codes imposed by the Taliban included severe restrictions on women's freedom of movement, expression and association. During this period, widespread human rights abuses committed by regional commanders of the Northern Alliance were not very publicised outside Afghanistan. Many of those commanders today hold powerful positions in the regions and in central government.

Now, . . . years after the end of the Taliban regime, the international community and the Afghan Transitional Administration (ATA), led by President Hamid Karzai, have proven unable to protect women. International human rights organisations and Afghan intellectuals are gravely concerned by the extent of violence faced by women and girls in Afghanistan now.

Sexual Violence

The risk of rape and sexual violence by members of armed factions and former combatants is still high. Forced marriage, particularly of underaged girls, and violence against women in the family are widespread in many areas of the country.

These crimes of violence continue with the active support or passive complicity of state agents, armed groups, families and communities. This continuing violence against women in Afghanistan causes untold suffering and denies women their fundamental human rights.

An Appalling Situation

The situation of women in Afghanistan remains appalling. Though girls and women in Kabul, and some other cities, are free to go to school and have jobs, this is not the case in most parts of the country. In the western province of Herat, the warlord Ismail Khan imposes Taliban-like decrees.

Many women have no access to education and are banned from working in foreign NGOs [nongovernmental organisations] or UN offices, and there are hardly any women in government offices. Women cannot take a taxi or walk in public unless accompanied by a close male relative. If seen with men who are not close relatives, women can be arrested by the "special police" and forced to undergo a hospital examination to see if they have recently had sexual intercourse. Because of this continued oppression, every month a large number of girls commit suicide—many more than under Taliban rule.

Women's rights fare no better in northern and southern Afghanistan, which are under the control of the Northern Alliance. According to an international NGO worker: "During the Taliban era, if a woman went to market and showed an inch of flesh she would have been beaten; but now she's getting raped."

According to Human Rights Watch, even in Kabul, where thousands of foreign troops are present, Afghan women do not feel safe and many continue to wear the burqa for protection. In some areas where girls' education does exist, parents are afraid to allow their daughters to take advantage of it, fol-

Prisoners in Their Own Homes

The rise of banditry and rape, often by the Afghan security authorities, has had a particularly devastating effect on women. Because the roads are not safe even in daylight, girls do not dare go to schools or their mothers to health centers. And when women are raped, they risk being murdered by their own families for besmirching the family honor.

"Many women and girls are essentially prisoners in their own homes," Human Rights Watch declared. And Amnesty International quoted an aid worker as saying: "During the Taliban era, if a woman went to market and showed an inch of flesh, she would have been flogged. Now she's raped."

Nicholas D. Kristof, New York Times, February 14, 2004.

lowing the burning down of several girls' schools. Girls have been abducted on the way to school and sexual assaults on children of both sexes are now very common.

Rhetoric Is Not Reality

In spite of its rhetoric, the Karzai government actively pursues policies that are anti-women.

Women cannot find jobs, and girls' schools often lack basic materials, such as books and chairs. There is no legal protection for women, and the legal systems prohibit them from getting help when they need it. Female singers are not allowed on Kabul television and women's songs are not played.

Karzai's government has established a women's ministry just to throw dust in the eyes of the international community. This ministry has done nothing for women and there are complaints that money given to the ministry by foreign NGOs has been taken by powerful warlords in the Karzai cabinet.

In addition, thousands of young Afghan women have been expelled from school simply because they are married. It's a big blow for female students, who were denied the right to education under the Taliban regime and hoped for more opportunities under the transitional administration.

A law passed in the mid-1970s that prohibited married women from attending high school was upheld by the government in September [2004], resulting in the expulsion of more than 3000 women students. Supporters of the legislation argue that the law protects unmarried girls from hearing explicit details about sex from married classmates.

The "war on terror" toppled the Taliban regime, but it has not removed religious radicalism and fanaticism, which is the main cause of misery for Afghan women. In fact, by bringing the warlords back to power, the US has replaced one anti-women, fundamentalist regime with another.

The US now supports the Northern Alliance, which was responsible for killing more than 50,000 civilians during its bloody rule in the 1990s. Those in power today are those who imposed anti-women restrictions as soon as they took control in 1992, after the resignation of President [Sayid] Najibullah. As soon as these armed militias came to power, they started a reign of terror throughout Afghanistan. Thousands of women and girls were systematically raped by militias and many committed suicide to avoid being sexually assaulted.

No Legal Protection

The criminal justice system does not offer effective protection for women. Prosecution for violence against women and protection for women at acute risk of violence is virtually absent. Those women who overcome the powerful barriers and seek redress are unlikely to have their complaints considered, or their rights defended.

Key donors supporting reform of the police and judiciary have failed to ensure that their intervention will support protection of women's rights. Protection and shelters for women at risk have not been created, and legal aid provision remains entirely inadequate.

It is vital that measures to protect the rights of women are built into legal and constitutional reform. We call on the Afghan Transitional Administration and the international community to act with urgency to protect women from violence and to build a criminal justice system that is able to defend women's right to live free from violence.

The prevailing insecurity has directly impacted on attempts by women to engage in political activities and ensure integration of women's rights in the process of reconstruction. Women delegates at the constitutional Loya Jirga (grand assembly meeting) were subject to intimidation. Human rights activists have a deep concern that women's participation in the coming election will be similarly threatened. The fake nature of the constitutional Loya Jirga and freedom of speech were clear to all the people of Afghanistan and the world in the attacks on the women delegates, Malalai Joya and Anar Kali.

Bill of Rights for Afghan Women

As a result of this Jirga, we have a so-called constitution that gives legitimacy to the tyrannical rule of warlords and is not able to protect women from violence and guarantee the protection of fundamental human rights and freedom. Therefore, I propose the creation and implementation of the following Bill of Rights for Afghan Women:

1. Mandatory education for women through secondary school and opportunities for all women for higher education.

2. Provision of up-to-date health services for women with special attention to reproductive rights.

3. Protection and security for women: the prevention and criminalization of sexual abuse and harassment against

71

women and children publicly and at home, domestic violence, and the use of women as compensation for crimes by one family against another so-called "bad blood-price".

4. Freedom of speech.

5. Freedom to vote and run for election to office.

6. Rights to marry and divorce, according to Islam.

7. Equal pay for equal work.

8. Right to financial independence and ownership of property.

9. Right to participate fully and to the highest levels in the economic and commercial life of the country.

10. Mandatory provision of economic opportunities for women.

11. Full representation of women in the Parliament.

12. Full inclusion of women in the judiciary system.

13. Minimum marriageable age set at 18 years.

14. Guarantee of all constitutional rights to widows, disabled women and orphans.

> *"[Under the Taliban,] women were denied education. . . . That tyranny has been replaced by . . . the power of freedom."*

Educational Opportunities Are Improving for Afghan Women

Laura Bush

According to Laura Bush in the following viewpoint, educational opportunities for Afghan women have greatly increased, particularly in Kabul, since the United States and its allies removed the fundamentalist Muslim Taliban from power in 2001. The creation of new educational facilities and programs will help bring education to girls in the rural provinces, which will help build a stronger democracy in which women play an equal part, she contends. Laura Bush is the First Lady of the United States.

As you read, consider the following questions:

1. According to the author, why is the establishment of a National Women's Dormitory important?
2. What are two vital needs of Afghan women, according to Bush?

Laura Bush, "Remarks at the Women's Teacher in Training Institute," Kabul, Afghanistan, March 30, 2005.

3. According to the author, what are some of the educational advances women have made since the Taliban regime was ousted?

It is, indeed, an extraordinary privilege to be with you today to celebrate the incredible progress that has been made by the people of Afghanistan over these past four years [since 2001]. I have especially watched with great pride as courageous women across your country have taken on leadership roles as teachers, students, doctors, judges, business and community leaders, and politicians. And nowhere is that more evident than on this University campus [the Women's Teacher Training Institute, Kabul, Afghanistan]. The United States Government is wholeheartedly committed to the full participation of women in all aspects of Afghan society, not just in Kabul, but in every province.

A Safe Place to Study

The National Women's Dormitory and the Women's Teacher Training Institute will allow women to come from every corner of the country and have a safe place to stay and study so that they can return home and share one of life's greatest gifts with their communities—the gift of an education.

I want to thank Mina Sherzoy, the Head of the Afghan Business Women's Council, for organizing the marketplace today which showcases some of the local wares being produced by women entrepreneurs. Mina recently led a delegation of 14 exceptional women entrepreneurs to the U.S. to participate in a mini-MBA [master of business administration] program spearheaded by Barbara Barrett and Thunderbird University—one of our nation's top international business schools. One of these exceptional women, Hamira Nassary, was my guest at President Bush's State of the Union address in the United States Capitol.

I would also like to thank Dr. Ashraf Ghani, the President of Kabul University for the opportunity to speak with you today. You are doing such important work and we greatly appreciate your devotion to the education of the people of Afghanistan.

Once a Dream; Now a Reality

It is said that big things have small beginnings. Two years ago [in 2003], the teacher training institute was just a dream. In July of 2003, the US-Afghan Women's Council visited one of my husband's top advisers, Karen Hughes, in her hometown of Austin, Texas. As Karen talked with them about the most pressing needs facing the women of Afghanistan, the consensus from her Afghan counterparts, including the Women's Minister, Habbiba Sarabi, was a dire need for teachers in the remote and rural communities. Karen was told that women hoping to attend the University did not have a place to stay. The dormitories had historically only been for men. Karen told me of these needs, and as a teacher and librarian myself, I hoped that the United States Government could help build this institute. Many of you here today have all played a critical role in making this dream a reality. And from today's small beginnings we expect the Institute will yield great things.

There is much more to this place than the bricks and mortar you see around us. The ordinary business that will take place here is, in fact, a symbol itself of the extraordinary leap forward Afghan women have taken.

A Young Democracy

We are only a few years removed from the rule of the terrorists, when women were denied education and every basic human right. That tyranny has been replaced by a young democracy, and the power of freedom is on display across Afghanistan.

We must be mindful though, that democracy is more than just elections. The survival of a free society ultimately depends on the participation of all its citizens, both men and women.

The Liberation of Afghan Women

In Afghanistan, the Taliban used violence and fear to deny Afghan women access to education, health care, mobility, and the right to vote. Our coalition has liberated Afghanistan and restored fundamental human rights and freedoms to Afghan women, and all the people of Afghanistan. Young girls in Afghanistan are able to attend schools for the first time.

George W. Bush, Women's Equality Day Proclamation,
August 23, 2002.

This is possible if institutions like this exist to give women the basic tools they need to contribute fully to society—and the most critical tool of all is an education.

So the hard work of the Institute has begun. Future teachers will come here for an innovative teacher training course. The Afghan Literacy Initiative, an accelerated literacy, math, and life skills curriculum for remote rural communities, where many girls still do not have access to schools, should have over 2,000 pupils by the end of [2005]. These students will be trained in their communities, as a result of a cascading system of training that begins with the development of the master trainers, here with us today.

Literacy and Health Care

Another program is Learning for Life, a health-focused course that is designed to help reduce maternal and child mortality. This program addresses two critical needs for Afghan women: literacy and health care. It will help people learn to read with materials that are focused on health. This makes literacy directly relevant to something women care about greatly—the well-being of their families. Over the next two years [2005–2007], Learning for Life will reach 8,000 women, and of those,

Stephane Peray. Reproduced by permission.

5,500 young women across thirteen provinces will qualify to be trained as health care workers and midwives.

The Teacher Training Institute is public-private partnership and it will continue to require the assistance of the Ministry of Education, numerous private donors, nongovernmental organizations, and of course, the U.S.-Afghan Women's Council.

I would so like to extend a special thanks to two United States corporations—Microsoft and Dell Computers—for their extraordinary generosity on behalf of both the Teacher Training Institute and the International Association of Women Judges. These companies heard that the women of Afghanistan had a need for technology assistance and they immediately provided computers, printers, and teaching application software. This is just one more example of the American people's commitment to the success of the people of Afghanistan.

Educating Future Leaders

Today I am proud to announce the United States' commitment to another initiative. The United States is supporting the establishment of the American University of Afghanistan with a multi-year commitment of more than 15 million dollars. This will provide a modern facility with an international faculty to educate future leaders.

The American University will aggressively reach out to young Afghan women, to ensure they feature prominently in the school and bring to it their invaluable perspective and determination. There will be appropriate facilities and housing for women, and care will be taken to be sure the faculty of this co-ed institution is inclusive of women. The school will also offer scholarships to outstanding young women who otherwise may not be able to attend. Classes will be offered in business, management, information technology, and other professional areas of study.

Finally, I'm pleased to announce the development of another education initiative—the International School of Afghanistan. The school will provide Afghan children from kindergarten through high school with a first-rate education through a classical curriculum including mathematics, language, literature and grammar, the sciences, social studies, culture and arts. We have dedicated $3.5 million for the establishment of this school.

These three initiatives are each significant. They are all part of an overall commitment by President Bush to Afghan education projects totaling 80 million dollars.

Equality for Women

These are more than just development projects—they also signify the bond between the American and Afghan people. They are symbols of our shared hopes and dreams for the future. That dream is of a prosperous, peaceful, and above all, a free

Afghanistan, where both men and women stand upright in equality.

As we have worked together these past years, we have accomplished much and launched projects that will yield great results in the coming years. We have also learned a great deal about each other. We have come to know what is in each other's hearts, and in so doing, come to understand that we are very much alike.

> "Decades of war . . . [have] badly affected the education sector and deprived a generation of the opportunity to be educated."

Educational Opportunities Are Not Improving for Afghan Women

Revolutionary Association of the Women of Afghanistan

In the following viewpoint the Revolutionary Association of the Women of Afghanistan (RAWA) states that a generation of girls in Afghanistan has been deprived of an education. Today, despite the claims of the United States and its allies, educational opportunities for Afghan women have not improved. The rulers of Afghanistan today treat women even worse than the fundamentalist Taliban did, according to RAWA. Unless the current government is removed from power, there will be no true educational opportunities for women in Afghanistan. RAWA is a political and social organization of Afghan women that struggles for peace, democracy, and women's rights.

As you read, consider the following questions:

1. According to RAWA, what was the Jihad Schoolbook Scandal?

Revolutionary Association of the Women of Afghanistan, "Speech by a RAWA member at the Conference on South Asian Education Systems," RAWA Web site, February 2, 2006. Reproduced by permission.

2. What has RAWA done to improve the education of Afghan girls, according to the author?

3. According to the author, why is it important that Afghan girls have access to free education?

RAWA is the oldest political/social organization of Afghan women, struggling for peace, freedom, democracy and women's rights in fundamentalism-blighted Afghanistan since 1977. Education has been the main focus and priority issue of RAWA, and we strongly believe that only the weapon of education can empower the women of Afghanistan to gain political awareness and participate actively in the struggle against fundamentalists. Because of this very fact, despite various problems and obstacles as well as insufficient resources, RAWA has taken the responsibility to administrate hundreds of literacy courses, schools and orphanages in Afghanistan and Pakistan based on its own teaching policy, promoting free-thinking and equality among all people regardless of gender, race or religion.

A Generation Deprived

In countries like Afghanistan, issues such as education cannot be understood without taking into account the whole political system. But no doubt, the decades of war from 1979 through the present has badly affected the education sector and deprived a generation of the opportunity to be educated. The puppet regime of Russia [the Soviet Union occupied Afghanistan from 1979 to 1989] destroyed our educational system in the name of democracy and women's rights. The fundamentalist Jehadis [Muslim religious warriors] . . . not only called doors of schools "gateways to hell", but also looted and burned books, schools and universities and kidnapped and raped hundreds of young school girls and women. The Taliban [the fundamentalist regime that ruled Afghanistan from 1996 to 2001] were the most misogynist and ignorant rulers, officially banning girls from studying at schools, universities and other

No Improvement

In truth, the situation of women in Afghanistan remains appalling. Though girls and women in Kabul, and some other cities, are free to go to school and have jobs, this is not the case in most parts of the country. In the western province of Herat, the warlord Ismail Khan imposes Taliban-like decrees. Many women have no access to education and are banned from working in foreign NGOs or UN offices, and there are hardly any women in government offices.

Mariam Rawi, Manchester (UK) Guardian, *February 12, 2004*

educational institutions; kept female teachers and doctors from their jobs and converted girls' schools into religious madrassas [Muslim schools].

The millions of Afghan refugees in Pakistan and Iran were the most deprived victims of war and fundamentalists' rule. In comparison to the 3 million refugees based in Pakistan, only a few thousand had access to education. Until recently there was no common educational policy. Fundamentalist Jehadi groups and NGOs [nongovernmental organizations] misused funds they received for the education of Afghan refugees. For instance, they would receive funds for 50,000 textbooks to be printed while they would only print 5,000 with very bad quality. More importantly, what was the mentality they were trying to build through their so-called education? Many textbooks were not of any use to the students, as books which were supposed to teach chemistry, biology, physics or Persian . . . were full of Hadis [Islamic sayings] and Quranic verses. The methods and language used in these books showed no understanding of students, their psychology or their well-being. Imagine children in first and second grade who were learn[ing] mathematics like this:

5 guns + 5 guns = 10 guns

Or, if a Muslim kills 5 infidels out of 10, how many will be left alive?

U.S. Support for Fundamentalists

And the shocking and painful fact is that from the very beginning, the US was the biggest supporter of fundamentalists in educational and cultural fields. As an example, [the U.S. oil company] Unocal paid $900,000 to the Center for Afghanistan Studies at the University of Omaha, Nebraska, to print textbooks promoting a fundamentalist vision. Two years ago [in 2004], USAID [U.S. Agency for International Development] reprinted through the same university, and these textbooks were no different from those earlier written by Jehadi groups. *The Washington Post* on March 23, 2002 disclosed only parts of the Jihad Schoolbook Scandal.

As an outcome of this critical situation, Afghanistan has one of the world's worst literacy rates, estimated by [the United Nations Children's Fund] UNICEF at between three to four percent for females and 28 percent for males.

Since once again the fundamentalist jehadis of the "Northern Alliance," [tribal alliance that opposed the Taliban] which have long been oppressors and violators of women's rights and education, are back in power with the support of the US and its allies, no radical change has happened in the economic, social, political and educational life of the people, particularly women. In order to deceive the outside world and make happy their masters, the "Northern Alliance" pays lip service to democracy and women's education . . . but their mentality and treatment of women is the same. The biggest threat to Afghan girl's education is the domination of "Northern Alliance" criminals. That is why in most provinces girls don't feel secure, are afraid of going outside their homes and rarely have access to educational institutions near their homes.

12-year-old Rahima, who was gang-raped in Takhar province on her way to school and girls like Muska who commit suicide to save their honor are clear examples of what life is like for Afghan girls under the Northern Alliance. In short, for the youth, especially school-going girls, life in Afghanistan is characterized by paralyzing physical danger. As a recently released report by Amnesty International explained, violence against females in the country is such that "daily Afghan women are at risk of abduction and rape by armed individuals. The government is doing little to improve their condition." Acts of violence against women are rarely investigated or punished.

Schools for Refugees

Since 1987, RAWA has established a number of schools for the refugee children to impart basic knowledge and modern thoughts that the fundamentalists have denied them. Though our schools were closed due to lack of funds in 1996, we are happy to say that with donations received from supporters around the world, RAWA opened around 15 schools in Pakistan. We also have hundreds of literacy courses for Afghan girls and women in almost all provinces of Afghanistan and in refugee camps in Pakistan.

During the Taliban period, RAWA, taking a great risk, managed to organize countless home-based classes throughout Afghanistan. Moreover, RAWA's orphanages offer safety, shelter, food, clothing and a better quality of education in many cities of Afghanistan and Pakistan for hundreds of children.

With further funds, RAWA hopes to establish schools equipped with laboratories, computers, halls, libraries and other modern facilities throughout Afghanistan.

Corruption

In order to provide all Afghans with good quality education, schools must remain free of cost from primary level up to university. Because of corrupt political and social system, our people are getting poorer and poorer every day. In such circumstances, talking about privatization of education or the establishment of private institutions will, at the end of the day, only fill foreigners' pockets and expand colonial culture. An American university will open in the near future where only warlord's children can study. Similarly, because both the ministry of foreign affairs and higher education and the embassies are in the hands of the criminal "Northern Alliance", scholarships never are given to the deserving students.

Afghanistan is still one of the poorest countries in the world. Just as its economic, cultural and social issues cannot be addressed without a radical change in the political system, its education is also a political phenomenon. By political change I mean the overthrow of the criminal warlord "Northern Alliance," whose power is the root cause of all the miseries and sufferings of our people. Until and unless these criminals are removed from political power, one can't hope for an essential change in the education sector.

Lastly I would like to say that only those governments, organizations and individuals are true friends of Afghan people who not only don't consider "Northern Alliance" their friends, but also strongly oppose them. We want you not to be deceived by their fashionable and stylish appearances or their speeches in the name of democracy and women's rights. Just as our people are suffering from the economic terror, political terror and social terror of the "Northern Alliance", to the same extent are they worried about education and the dark fate that is waiting for them without it. This is not only RAWA's message, but it is the voice of our people, who want the world to hear them and join hands with them in their struggle against the enemies of democracy, freedom and peace.

> *"Warlords, fueled with new weaponry and American dollars to fight the War on Terror, now have the capacity to terrorize the women of Afghanistan again."*

Violence Against Afghan Women Has Increased

Aisha Ahmad

Aisha Ahmad argues in the following viewpoint that Afghan women were safer under the rule of the fundamentalist Taliban regime than they are today. Since the U.S. invasion that toppled the Taliban, Ahmad contends, warlords now control much of the country, and violent sexual assaults on women are now common again. Afghan women are pleased that the Taliban regime is gone, but they hope that the fledgling democratic institutions will eventually provide safety and security for them. Aisha Ahmad is conducting research on the disarmament of warlords in post-Taliban Afghanistan.

As you read, consider the following questions:

1. According to Ahmad, how has rape been used as a weapon in Afghanistan?

Aisha Ahmad, "Behind the Purdah: Wartime Sexual Violence in Afghanistan," http://www.cbc.ca, May 26, 2005. Reproduced by permission.

2. Why were women safer under the Taliban regime, according to the author?

3. According to Ahmad, why is the government of Afghanistan unable to protect women?

For over two decades of war and inter-ethnic strife, women in Afghanistan have hidden in the shame of rape and sexual violence. In a country where more than 80 per cent of women are illiterate and live in remote rural areas, stories of wartime rape are veiled within the secret world of the *purdah*, the traditional barrier in Afghan society that keeps women separated from public life.

But from the uncomfortable silence, Afghan women across the country shared with me their experiences under the threat of sexual violence.

Systematic Rape

During Afghanistan's civil war period in the early 1990s, warlords and militiamen ravaged the countryside using systematic rape campaigns against rival factions. Diana Hashimzada, an Uzbek from the ethnically divided city of Mazar e Sharif, recalled, "Before the Taliban came, there were many commanders from each ethnicity. Hazara militiamen raped Tajik women, Tajik militias raped Uzbek women, and Uzbeks raped Pashtuns ... whenever a militiaman would find a woman of another ethnicity, he would rape her."

Women from the ultra-conservative and Pashtun-dominated southern region of the country had similar stories. "The militiamen would go into the houses and tie up the men. They would rape the women in front of their brothers, husbands and fathers and then leave," said Yasmine, a 24-year-old rural health worker from Kandahar.

"When I was in Zabul province, we had a young man shoot himself in the head because he had watched his sister get raped by militia gangs and could not live with the shame."

Continued Abuse

Afghanistan is in the process of reconstruction after many years of conflict, but hundreds of thousands of women and girls continue to suffer abuse at the hands of their husbands, fathers, brothers, armed individuals, parallel legal systems, and institutions of the state itself such as the police and the justice system. There are reported increases in forced marriages; some women in difficult situations have even killed themselves to escape such a heinous situation whilst others burn themselves to death to draw attention to their plight.

Amnesty International, May 30, 2005

Victims

Practically every woman I encountered in Afghanistan was either a victim of rape herself or personally knew someone affected by sexual violence during the civil war period. These old scars have left a mark of violence and fear on Afghan women. The Taliban actually enjoyed a short-lived popularity in 1996, when they expelled the warlords from the countryside.

Ironically, even though the Taliban were infamous for their tyrannical policies on female education, employment and mobility, my discussions with women in the northern, central and southern regions of Afghanistan revealed that the Taliban regime, through its strict interpretations of Islamic law, virtually eliminated the ethnic rape campaigns and widespread sexual violence.

"During the Taliban we could not come to the [health] clinic without our husbands and we could not move around freely, but there was no threat of rape for women," said Ayesha, 40, a Pashtun villager from rural Kandahar province.

"The Taliban made it so that no one could come into our homes. A woman could even sleep with her door open at night and nothing would happen to her."

A Reduction in Sexual Violence

Even in the ethnically fragmented northern province of Balkh, women noticed a reduction in sexual violence under the Taliban regime. Twenty-year-old widow Akala, from Khoja Ghalak village, struggled to feed herself and her two children during the Taliban regime, but says she was under no threat of sexual violence.

"Under the Taliban, I was not able to work in the field or go to the bazaar, or even visit the cemetery to pray. I am a widow, so my life was extremely difficult. But [the Taliban] never went into houses or violated women. They were very good people in that regard.

"The only restriction was that you couldn't go outside, or even think about going outside. They killed a lot of people, but they did not rape women. And the men were all afraid to rape because the Taliban would kill them."

Since the fall of the Taliban government women have resumed their positions in the public life of Afghanistan, as girls eagerly returned to schools and universities, and professional women re-entered the workforce. However, the defeat of the Taliban has come at the enormous cost of justice for many silenced rape victims.

The Northern Alliance

From the start of the War on Terror, the American military joined forces with the anti-Taliban Northern Alliance militias under the leadership of commanders such as General Rashid Dostum and Mohammad Atta, who are known to have propagated ethnically-motivated rape campaigns during the civil war period.

These warlords, fuelled with new weaponry and American dollars to fight the War on Terror, now have the capacity to terrorize the women of Afghanistan again.

"Before the Taliban, General Dostum did many injustices to women," says Akala. "Now he is away in Kabul where President [Hamid] Karzai and the Americans are controlling him . . . but we have no regard for Dostum."

Foreign Occupation

As long as the international community keeps its eyes on Afghanistan, many local people believe that the warlords can be kept in check. Most Afghans accept foreign occupation because they realize that these newly reinstated warlords are again powerful enough to wage another civil war.

Abdul Qadir Noorzai, director of the Afghan Independent Human Rights Commission in Kandahar, noted the fragility of the current peace.

"Right now there are external forces controlling Afghanistan. The Afghan National Army is not strong enough to keep the peace. When General Dostum refused to accept the central authority, only the Americans, under threat of force, could bring him back to Kabul. If the international presence leaves Afghanistan, the situation here will collapse within a month."

The Government's Inability to Protect Women

But controlling the warlords brings no justice to the victims of sexual violence in Afghanistan, and the Karzai government has already demonstrated a total inability to protect the security of women and children.

Northern Alliance warlords, once ousted by the Taliban, have now resumed effective military and economic control of the countryside. While the Karzai administration struggles to build a new national army, district level commanders maintain de facto control over their private fiefdoms.

The government in Kabul holds no influence whatsoever outside of Afghanistan's major urban centers, leaving rural security in the hands of militias.

Abida, a schoolteacher in Kandahar, was forced to leave her teaching position under the Taliban regime. But although she is now able to resume her work at the school, Abida complained of a sharp rise in sexual violence during Karzai's period in office.

"My daughter was taken by gunpoint and raped. She has a small baby now and they are living with me. She has tried to kill herself many times by setting herself on fire. Her rapist is walking freely through the streets of Kandahar and nothing can be done.

"There are many other Afghan women like my daughter who are killing themselves and burning themselves alive because of this shame. It's no longer safe to walk alone in the streets."

Hope in Democracy

However, despite the re-emerging threat of sexual violence, women unanimously applauded the fall of the Taliban, and pointed to the emerging democratic process and developing central government as the only solution to Afghanistan's lawlessness. Weary and impoverished, women have been the frontline victims of war for over two decades and are hungry for stability and effective government.

While the fledgling Karzai administration seems to be more concerned with solidifying diplomatic and military relations with the United States, than with fostering a sense of security and confidence in the central government in the rural areas. The female vote constituted over 40% of the Afghan electorate in the presidential election . . . , but women in rural areas in the south complained that the central government has no power to control local commanders and power holders.

But while the burden of shame falls on the shoulders of Afghan women, the international community should look at the new regime they have created for Afghanistan. In a country where warlords and rapists rule with impunity, Afghan women continue to be denied their rights to freedom and justice.

Periodical Bibliography

The following articles have been selected to supplement the diverse views presented in this chapter.

Aryn Baker and
Bamiyan Muhib
Habibi

"A Woman's Place: Four Years After the Fall of the Taliban, Afghan Women Are Now Guaranteed a Role in Government. Can They Save a Nation Still Groping for Peace?" *Time International* (Asia Edition), September 19, 2005.

Babak
Dehghanpisheh

"Now, the Hard Part: Afghan Women Have Come a Long Way Since the Days of the Taliban. But the Rights They've Won Are More Fragile than Ever," *Newsweek International*, October 4, 2002.

Sonali Kolhatkar

"Afghan Women Continue to Fend for Themselves," *Foreign Policy in Focus*, March 9, 2004.

Christina Lamb

"The Return of the Taliban: Liberated Women? The Chief Justice Wants to Ban Women from Driving," *New Statesman*, March 22, 2004.

Saad Mohseni and
Don Ritter

"Empowering Afghan Women," *Washington Times*, May 5, 2005.

Ron Moreau and
Sami Yousafzai

"Living Dead No More: The Women of the Afghan Capital Are Thriving," *Newsweek*, October 11, 2004.

Masuda Sultan

"Afghan Constitution a Partial Victory for Women," January 14, 2004. www.womenwaging peace.net.

Juliette Terzieff

"Out of the House and Back to School—Afghan Girls and Young Women Are Returning to School in Record Numbers," *World and I*, October 2002.

Priya Verma

"Afghanistan: Women Candidates Attacked," *Off Our Backs*, July/August 2005.

CHAPTER 3

How Should Drug Production in Afghanistan Be Addressed?

Chapter Preface

Immediately following the ousting of the Taliban regime in 2001, the cultivation of poppies in Afghanistan decreased. However, production slowly resumed and then sharply increased in 2003. Since then, American officials have frequently condemned Afghan poppy production and encouraged Afghan authorities to prevent it. Many analysts maintain that eradication of Afghan poppy crops would certainly reduce heroin use in the United States. Others, however, argue that as long as there is demand, poppies will be cultivated in Afghanistan.

The trend in the United States in recent years suggests that heroin production will continue to be a lucrative business because demand in America continues to grow. According to the 2005 National Drug Assessment Summary Report, in 2003 more than 310,000 people aged twelve and over in the United States reported using heroin in the previous year. Perhaps an even more accurate indicator of the scope of the heroin problem is the number of people who seek treatment for addiction. Between 1992 and 2002, the number of people admitted to publicly funded treatment facilities for heroin addiction increased from 168,321 to 285,667—an increase of 170 percent. Notably, this increase occurred before the surge in heroin production in Afghanistan that began in 2003, undermining the claim that production drives consumption.

Some analysts claim that the superior quality of the heroin being produced in Afghanistan today is responsible for the increase in the drug's use. High-quality heroin can be snorted or smoked, which appeals to many people put off by intravenous drug use. According to Susan M. Gordon, director of research at the Caron Foundation, a leading drug treatment center, the increase in heroin use is the result of an increase in snorting or smoking heroin rather than injecting it. "Earlier heroin epidemics were based on intravenous use," she states. "But the more recent availability of inexpensive and very pure heroin allows users to sniff or smoke it—rather than inject it—which has led to wider use."

Another result of the availability of cheaper, purer Afghan heroin is that the profile of the typical user has changed considerably. "The user of today is not the user of the 1970s," says Kathleen Kane-Willis, assistant director of Roosevelt University's Institute for Metropolitan Affairs. "The user of today defies the traditional stereotype of being minority, urban, male and poor. What I've seen in the Chicago area is there is a rise in middle-class users." Gordon concurs: "Almost 90 percent of recent admissions to Caron's adult treatment programs are white and have a high school diploma or higher level of education. More than 50 percent are employed full-time."

Impoverished Afghan farmers continue to grow poppies because it is the most profitable crop they can grow. Unless demand for heroin in the West declines, many commentators assert, it is unreasonable to expect that the supply of cheap, pure Afghan heroin will be eliminated.

> "President Karzai is determined to pro-
> ceed with every major aspect of break-
> ing the heroin trade."

Efforts to End Illegal Drug Production in Afghanistan Will Succeed

Robert B. Charles

In the following viewpoint Robert B. Charles argues that the U.S. and Afghan governments have developed a comprehensive counternarcotics strategy to curtail heroin production in Afghanistan. Poppies must be eradicated, alternative sources of income developed, and law enforcement capabilities must be enhanced, he contends. With the help of European allies, efforts to end illegal drug production in Afghanistan will succeed, according to Charles. Robert B. Charles was assistant secretary of state for international narcotics and law enforcement affairs from 2003 to 2005.

As you read, consider the following questions:

1. According to the author, what are Afghan president Hamid Karzai's goals regarding drug production?

Robert B. Charles, "Afghanistan: The Narcotics Situation and Strategy," http://www.state.gov/g/inl/rls/rm/29888.htm, February 26, 2004. U.S. Department of State, Washington, D.C.

2. How is heroin production connected to terrorism, according to Charles?

3. In the author's opinion, what can European nations contribute to the war on drugs in Afghanistan?

The U.S. Government strategy for dealing with narcotics both within Afghanistan and trafficked from it is proactive and coordinated within the interagency. It is intended to measurably reduce heroin poppy cultivation, encourage alternative income streams, destroy drug labs, promote drug interdiction, and develop the justice sector to facilitate the proper prosecution and sentencing of traffickers. This State Department Bureau, the Bureau for International Narcotics and Law Enforcement Affairs (INL), is intent on working closely and effectively with both Congress and DEA [Drug Enforcement Administration] to implement this strategy. In fact, the DEA Administrator and I have returned from a fact-finding trip to Afghanistan, where we represented the U.S. Government at the counter-drug conference in Kabul [in February 2004].

A Comprehensive Counternarcotics Strategy

Pieces of this counternarcotics strategy are proportionate to the urgency and needs presented on the ground. The various pieces of this emerging strategy are both complementary and independently important; the key words are proactive, comprehensive, and accountable.

A few first impressions. My meeting with President [Hamid] Karzai reaffirmed my conviction that he means business—he is serious about tackling the heroin threat to his country. This is a leader who is dedicated to breaking the cycle of opium poppy cultivation and narcotics trafficking in his country before local trafficking rings become cartels and put down taproots, transforming Afghanistan into a narco-state. President Karzai is determined to proceed with every major aspect of breaking the heroin trade, even as he rein-

Free of Poppies

[In May 2004], the southeastern Afghan province of Nangrahar was covered with pink and white poppies, producing a quarter of the nation's opium crop. [In May 2005,] after President Hamid Karzai announced a jihad, or holy war, against drugs, Nangrahar is almost 80 percent free of poppies.

Scott Baldauf, Christian Science Monitor, *May 16, 2005*

forces the productivity of alternative legitimate income streams, such as through the production of wheat, maize, barley and other needed crops.

Eradicating Poppies

As you know well, there are three essential components to our accelerating counter-narcotics strategy. The first component is targeted eradication of heroin poppies. The second is targeted, ever-widening availability and reinforcement of alternative streams of income. Democracies are consolidated not by reliance on drug money, but by pairing well-supported democratic institutions and the rule of law with a sound, growing, and free market in legitimate goods. Afghanistan has great needs, for example, in the area of legitimate agriculture. We intend to support the growth of a legitimate economy in that and other sectors.

Third, and finally, law enforcement, interdiction and justice sector reform are also key to success. We must raise the costs and risks of heroin trafficking, while raising the incentives for joining, or remaining part of, the legitimate economy. Only eight percent of Afghanistan's cultivated land is presentlused to grow poppies, and we must make the incremental risk of its associated profits higher than the extra income it might produce.

There are other dangers from which we cannot avert our gaze. Afghanistan's heroin, which sells on the retail market for one hundred times the farm gate price, is the source of a growing reservoir of illegal money that funds international crime across the region, sustains the destabilizing activities of warlords, and fosters local coercion and terrorism. While available information about this pattern continues to grow, we cannot afford to stand by and wait as these destructive relationships and behaviors become clearer and institutionalized. Our comprehensive approach takes stock of these linkages, and is accelerating the effort to break each of them. . . .

On eradication, some would argue—wait. Other priorities should trump this activity. I would argue swift action is essential. Distinguishing the urgent from the otherwise important requires that we tackle the poppy crop now.

A Committed Ally

Second, I can say without qualification that we have a committed ally in the Afghan government. President Karzai believes in democracy, the rule of law and human rights, and in a robust counter-narcotics effort. I see no signs of half-measures, and we are similarly committed.

Third, I am convinced that drug money and terrorist organizations in Afghanistan and throughout the region are locked together like chain links. While there may be other links in that chain, it is my conviction, based on the information available, that the two threats overlap palpably and incontrovertibly.

Fourth, we are cooperating closely with our European allies to support the Afghan government, particularly those with lead nation responsibilities. In that regard, we are pressing for increasing coordination with the British on counter-narcotics; with the Germans on policing; and with the Italians on justice sector reform.

Fifth, and finally, INL is determined to support and encourage cooperation between the efforts of the State Department, DEA, DoD [Department of Defense], and USAID [U.S. Agency for International Development]. Congress empowers us to achieve results for the American people, for the Afghan people and for greater local, regional and national security. Congress has funded the INL-coordinated portion of that effort with $50 million in supplemental appropriations in Fiscal Year 2004, of which a significant portion will be dedicated to eradication.

Police Training

Separately, Congress has funded INL police training and criminal justice sector development with an additional $120 million in 2004 supplemental funds, to which the [Bush] Administration added $50 million in reprogrammed funds for accelerating success in Afghanistan, after appropriately notifying the Congress. Of this $170 million, $160 million is being used to build 7 police training centers to train at least 20,000 police by June [2004], and $10 million is to develop the justice sector, including the training of judges and prosecutors, the building of courthouses, and the reinforcement of the rule of law through guidance on developing new laws, and the provision of technical assistance.

In short, we are seeking to prevent the institutionalization of heroin cartels, to support democracy's early days in post-Taliban Afghanistan, to reinforce the best instincts of a people now freeing themselves from the terrorists' yoke, and to confront those that still threaten to destabilize that society, through both the narcotics trade and terrorism.

We Will Succeed

This effort means being active in containing the narcotics trafficking threats in places like Turkmenistan, Uzbekistan, Tajikistan, the Kyrgyz Republic, Kazakhstan, and Pakistan, as well as points South and West. It means working with the United Nations office on Drugs and Crime (UNODC), strengthening our cooperation with DEA, focusing work with the G-8's June 2003 endorsement of the "Paris Pact" to zero-in on "drug routes" from Afghanistan to heroin markets, and demonstrating global leadership through our own efforts. . . .

INL is involved in a full-court press on both counter-narcotics and law enforcement in and around Afghanistan. These issues will not vanish overnight, but with congressional support and bipartisan cooperation in the knowledge that success in Afghanistan matters, we will, incrementally and collectively, succeed.

"*No matter whom you listen to, . . . the drug war in Afghanistan is a bust.*"

Efforts to End Illegal Drug Production in Afghanistan Will Fail

Robert B. Scheer

In the following viewpoint Robert B. Scheer argues that the George W. Bush administration's claims of success at eliminating drug production in Afghanistan are deceptive. In fact, Afghanistan is now a narco-state, Scheer claims, and efforts to eliminate heroin production in that nation have failed. Scheer contends that America is not even trying to abolish the heroin trade in Afghanistan. Robert Scheer is a senior lecturer at the Annenberg School of Communications at the University of Southern California.

As you read, consider the following questions:

1. According to Scheer, who is really in charge of Afghanistan?

2. How widespread is poppy cultivation in Afghanistan, according to the author?

3. As related by Scheer, how is terrorism connected to illegal drug distribution?

Why am I such a party pooper? Trust me, I desperately want to be like those happy-go-lucky folks in the red [conservative] states who apparently think things are hurtling along just fine. Unfortunately, the facts keep bridling my optimism.

Take the United States' alleged great achievements in Afghanistan. Remember during the [2004 presidential election] campaign how President Bush repeatedly celebrated the divinely inspired success of his administration toward turning Afghanistan into a stable democracy? "In Afghanistan, I believe that the freedom there is a gift from the Almighty," he said in the third presidential debate. "And I can't tell you how encouraged I am to see freedom on the march." As compared with Iraq, which Jon Stewart's "The Daily Show" has aptly titled "Mess-O-Potamia," Afghanistan has claimed fewer American lives and taxpayer dollars, while managing to hold a presidential election since U.S. and warlord irregulars deposed the brutal Taliban regime [in 2001].

Sure, we haven't captured [terrorist leader] Osama bin Laden or the Taliban's Mullah Mohammed Omar, and 20,000 young American soldiers are rather miserably stationed there, but who am I to nitpick when faced with the stirring sight of democracy abloom?

The Opium Economy

Well, truth is, freedom in Afghanistan continues to be on more of a stoned-out stumble than a brisk march. The Taliban has been driven from Kabul, but it still exists in the countryside, and the bulk of the country is still run, de facto, by competing warlords dependent on the opium trade, which now accounts for 60% of the Afghan economy.

"The fear that Afghanistan might degenerate into a narco-state is slowly becoming a reality," said the executive director

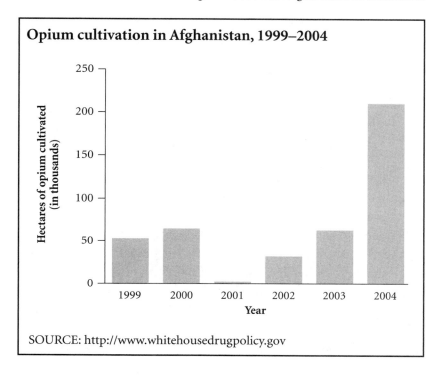

Opium cultivation in Afghanistan, 1999–2004

SOURCE: http://www.whitehousedrugpolicy.gov

of the United Nations' Office on drugs and Crime, Antonio Maria Costa. "Opium cultivation, which has spread like wild-fire . . . could ultimately incinerate everything: democracy, reconstruction and stability."

Costa's office has just released a slew of discouraging numbers that lay out in numbing detail how Afghanistan's opium production has soared in the last year to an all-time high. The raw form of heroin is now the staple crop in every province, while in just one year the area under poppy cultivation has increased 64%. The country produces 87% of the world's opium, and one out of 10 Afghans is employed by the illicit industry, according to the alarming U.N. report.

Of course, brandishing quotes from the U.N. doesn't sit well with isolationist yahoos. So, for them, here are highlights from the White House's own Office of National Drug Control Policy report, which painted an even darker picture: "Current [Afghan opium] cultivation levels equate to a . . . 239% increase in the poppy crop and a 73% increase in potential opium production over 2003 estimates"—a sixfold increase in the three years since the Taliban was driven from Kabul.

Failures

No matter whom you listen to, then, the drug war in Afghanistan is a bust. Unfortunately, both the U.N. and the White House have repeatedly said the drug war and the war on terror are nearly synonymous, especially in Afghanistan, where drug money has long directly and indirectly aided and abetted extremists such as Al Qaeda.

Indeed, this administration came into office preoccupied by the war on drugs and indifferent to the war on terror. Before [the September 11, 2001, terrorist attacks], even though Afghanistan was harboring the world's No. 1 terror suspect and his organization [Osama bin Laden and al Qaeda], the White House was so happy with the Taliban regime's drug-trade crackdown that Secretary of State Colin Powell announced in May 2001 that the U.S. was extending $43 million in humanitarian aid to Kabul, under U.N. auspices, as a reward.

Opium Haze

Now that it has the war on terror as a perfect excuse for such wildly risky fantasies as the wholesale remaking of the Middle East at gunpoint, winning the drug war in Afghanistan is no longer even on the White House's radar. Never mind that the drug trade is booming in Afghanistan and those who harbored Bin Laden and Al Qaeda are regrouping.

In the opium haze that threatens to swallow up Afghanistan's vaunted rebirth, it is only the illusion of progress—not progress itself—that is being sold. Because the president has presented all this as a wonderful dream instead of a nightmare that Afghanistan has had before, it raises the question: Just what is *he* smoking?

> "Licensing production of legitimate drugs would ... provide a sustainable livelihood for the poor peasants and generate income for the Afghan state."

Afghanistan Should Use Poppies to Produce Legal Medicines

Vanda Felbab-Brown

Vanda Felbab-Brown argues in the following viewpoint that licensing the cultivation of poppies to make legal drugs such as morphine could be a solution to Afghanistan's illegal drug trade. The current method of trying to eradicate the poppies would harm farmers and decimate the country's economy. A pilot program in which some poppy growers are licensed should be studied as a way to eliminate illegal drug production in Afghanistan. Vanda Felbab-Brown is a fellow at the Belfer Center for Science and International Affairs at Harvard University's Kennedy School of Government.

As you read, consider the following questions:

1. According to Felbab-Brown, where has licensing of legitimate medicine production with poppies worked?

Vanda Felbab-Brown, "Afghanistan and Opium," *Boston Globe*, December 18, 2005. Reproduced by permission.

2. How could the United States guarantee sufficient income for farmers growing poppies for legal medicines, according to Felbab-Brown?

3. As stated by the author, how large is the demand for pain-relief medications?

A UN [United Nations] report on drugs in Afghanistan points to the success of eradication in decreasing the area under poppy cultivation by 21 percent during [2005]. Yet this positive development is fragile and likely unsustainable. Instead of doctrinally clinging to eradication, the international community should explore other means of decreasing Afghanistan's illicit economy, such as converting the still vast opium cultivation into legal production for medical opiates.

Why Not Afghanistan?

The idea of transforming the cultivation for the production of codeine and morphine is promoted by the Senlis Council, a European drug policy think tank. Pointing to the successful implementation of such a scheme in Turkey, where it eliminated the large illegal cultivation of opium, the Senlis advocates ask: Why not Afghanistan?

Licensing production of legitimate drugs would not only shrink the size of Afghanistan's illegal economy, it would also provide a sustainable livelihood for the poor peasants and generate income for the Afghan state.

Eradication or opium production has been the method of choice for fighting the illegal drug trade thus far, but it is socially explosive since the poor farmers do not have an alternative source of livelihood. Even in the best case of eradication working, this would mean the elimination of 40 percent of Afghanistan's gross domestic product.

Licensing is not a perfect solution either. It would be difficult to keep licensed farmers from selling their opium to drug dealers for higher prices. The International Narcotics Control

Board [INCB] that regulates exports of medical opiates, and the narcotics treaties that permit the legal cultivation of opium poppy for domestic medical opiates, require government monopoly of the system in order to keep the opium from falling into the wrong hands. Given the poor security conditions in Afghanistan, the Afghan government would have a hard time enforcing the regulations on farmers.

A Pilot Program

But these challenges should not keep a pilot program from being attempted. For instance, private contractors could be hired not to spray illicit crops, but to monitor and patrol the areas of legal production. Compliance could also be reinforced by working with traditional Afghan tribal structures. Realistically, some diversion into the illegal market must be expected. However, diversion smaller than the current 100 percent "diversion" into the illegal market is a step in the right direction.

Another challenge is what to do with farmers who are not issued a license. Eradicating opium crops of unlicensed farmers would help deter licensed farmers from diverting their opium into illegal traffic, but it would also generate tensions among groups and tribes that benefit more than others from the licensing scheme. To maintain stability and still reduce illicit cultivation, it would be better to focus on apprehending traffickers and busting the labs, while working toward enhancing state law enforcement capacity and enlarging licensed areas.

How much of the illicit economy could ultimately be absorbed for medicinal uses would also depend on the demand for medical opiates. One of the reasons why the licensing scheme has been successful in Turkey is that the United States guarantees a market for Turkish (as well as Indian) medical opiates. Under the so-called "80–20" rule . . . the United States agrees to buy at least 80 percent of medical opiates from Turkey and India. Together with Australia, Turkey and India are

A Potentially Merciful Crop

The United States wants Afghanistan to destroy its potentially merciful crop, which has increased sevenfold since 2002 and now constitutes 60 percent of the country's gross domestic product. But why not bolster the country's stability and end both the pain and the trafficking problems by licensing Afghanistan with the International Narcotics Control Board to sell its opium legally?

Maia Szalavitz, New York Times, *July 13, 2005.*

the world's largest suppliers of legal opiates. Turkey and India would, of course, object to the "80–20 rule" being altered to accommodate Afghanistan. In addition, if they lost their market share, the odds for more of their crops ending up on the illegal market [would] increase.

The INCB contends that there should be a balance between demand and supply and that currently there is no space for Afghanistan's medical opiates. The Senlis Council contends that there is a need in developing countries, where millions suffer from HIV/AIDS and cancers without any pain-relief medications.

Yet under the highly regulated market of medical opiates, bureaucratic barriers to distributing these drugs keep any such arrangement from happening quickly. Between need and demand, there is regulation.

Providing Hope

However, a creative design of the US foreign aid bill could combine money ear-marked for counternarcotics efforts and for efforts to fight AIDS to purchase Afghanistan's legal opium for distribution among AIDS patients in the developing world.

Granted there are potential problems, but a licensing system in Afghanistan should be explored. It would provide hope for alleviating poverty in Afghanistan and suffering of others, as well as promise lucrative rewards for pharmaceutical firms.

| "It will take time for a democratic Afghanistan to eliminate opium production."

Afghanistan Should Gradually Curtail Poppy Cultivation

Peter Reuter and Victoria Greenfield

Peter Reuter and Victoria Greenfield argue in the following viewpoint that the United States was initially too forceful in its demands that Afghan president Hamid Karzai be more aggressive in his efforts to curtail illegal poppy cultivation. Drastic actions to eliminate Afghanistan's poppy crop would have further impoverished the country and weakened the government. The United States should continue to support Afghanistan in its efforts to gradually curtail the production of illegal drugs. Peter Reuter is a professor in the School of Public Policy and Department of Criminology at the University of Maryland; Victoria Greenfield is a senior economist at the Rand Corporation, a public policy think tank based in Santa Monica, California.

As you read, consider the following questions:

1. According to the authors, what indicates that the United States has changed its position on Afghanistan's methods of eliminating illegal drug production?

Peter Reuter and Victoria Greenfield, "Outside View: Opium and Democracy," *UPI*, May 4, 2005. Copyright © 2005 by United Press International. Reproduced by permission.

2. Why is a harsh crackdown on Afghan opium growers not appropriate, according to Reuter and Greenfield?

3. In the authors' opinion, why are the cases of Thailand and Pakistan good models for Afghan poppy eradication?

When Secretary of State Condoleezza Rice stood beside Afghan President Hamid Karzai, she made an enlightened statement about cutting Afghanistan's opium production, saying: "It is a problem that took a while to develop, and it will take time to end the problem."

Rice's statement in March [2005] is the clearest confirmation yet of a gradual turn in U.S. policy since early 2004, when the Bush administration and Congress were calling for an immediate crackdown on Afghanistan's biggest cash crop. Her statement shows the United States' new patience and acceptance that it will take time for a democratic Afghanistan to eliminate opium production.

An Impossible Task

When the United States earlier pushed Karzai to immediately end opium production in his war-torn country—without instituting the repressive tactics that historically have led to rapid success—the United States was giving the Afghan leader a virtually impossible task. Afghanistan could please the United States only by aggressive action that would further impoverish its already poor population and undermine the government's legitimacy.

The Taliban announced a ban on growing poppies—the source of opium—in Afghanistan in July 2000, saying this reflected the teachings of the Koran. Already feared by Afghans for its brutality, the Taliban achieved compliance with its poppy ban by tearing up the fields of a few early producers who violated the ban, thereby showing that the government was serious.

An Alternative Future

In the long term, success demands that average Afghans understand why we must defeat the narcotics industry—for our country, for our faith and for our children. But poppy farmers will accept the loss of their livelihoods only if they believe in an alternative future, and if they see commensurate punishments for those at the top of the drug pyramid.

Ashraf Ghani, New York Times, *December 11, 2004.*

The result of the Taliban's order was a dramatic reduction in Afghan opium production, which fell from 3,600 tons in 2000 to just 185 tons in 2001. This caused world opium production to fall by more than 60 percent.

This wasn't the first time that large and rapid reductions in opium production have been achieved by massive government repression.

Police Crackdowns

When the Communists took power in China in 1949, the nation was a major opium producer and suffered from what may have been the world's worst opium consumption problem. Within two years of a police crackdown on opium production and consumption—resulting in mass executions and imprisonments—opium production and use had essentially disappeared in China.

The Islamic Revolution in 1979 in Iran used some of the same police-state tactics as China to eliminate the large production and consumption of opium that had prevailed under the rule of the shah of Iran.

There may be yet another, slightly less dramatic instance of successful reduction. Myanmar, formerly known as Burma, is the world's second-largest producer of opium. A rebel movement, the United Wa State Army, has control of the major poppy-growing areas and has already reduced production by three-quarters in the past six years, with a realistic promise to end production by June [2005]. It has accomplished this mostly by forcible relocation of some 100,000 peasant farming families who grow poppies.

Unacceptable in a Democracy

But if Afghanistan's current government resorted to the tactics of the Taliban, the Chinese Communists, Iran's dictatorship and the rebels in Myanmar to end opium production, it would rightly be condemned by the United States and other democratic nations. This is because in each of the successful crackdowns on opium, authorities relied on methods that are simply not acceptable in a democratic nation, no matter how noble the purpose.

The success of anti-opium campaigns in more politically open settings is much more gradual. Thailand, once a major world opium producer, is the leading example. A combination of general economic development and targeted programs—both crop substitution and law enforcement—led Thailand to almost end its opium production over a period of more than a decade. Pakistan, also a formerly significant producer, has managed to almost entirely exit opium production over a similar period, notwithstanding a recent upturn in poppy harvests.

Going after traffickers rather than farmers, albeit politically much more acceptable, is even more difficult. Few governments, authoritarian or otherwise, have had a high degree of success in this arena. While ending poppy production, Iran and Pakistan are still major drug traffickers. The recent Thai crackdown, with the extra-judicial killing of 2,000 drug dealers in less than a year, seems to have lessened domestic drug use but does not offer a helpful model for a democracy-building Afghanistan.

Patience

Secretary Rice's call for patience in the fight against opium production in Afghanistan shows an acceptance of the dilemma Afghanistan faces and is an encouraging indication that the U.S. government has learned from history.

Periodical Bibliography

The following articles have been selected to supplement the diverse views presented in this chapter.

Robert Charles	"The Afghan Dilemma," *Washington Times*, April 26, 2005.
Dexter Filkins	"Afghanistan to Pay Farmers for Uprooted Poppies," *New York Times*, April 5, 2002.
Ashraf Ghani	"Where Democracy's Greatest Enemy Is a Flower," *New York Times*, December 11, 2004.
Andre Hollis	"A War on Drugs and Terror," *Washington Times*, January 14, 2004.
Christian Parenti	"Afghan Poppies Bloom: The War-Ravaged, Opium-Dependent Country Lives in Fear of a New Drug War," *Nation*, January 24, 2005.
Eric Schmitt	"Afghans' Gains Face Big Threat in Drug Traffic," *New York Times*, December 11, 2004.
Maia Szalavitz	"Let a Thousand Licensed Poppies Bloom," *New York Times*, July 13, 2005.
Amy Waldman	"A Village at Source of Heroin Trade Fears the Eradication of Its Poppies," *New York Times*, March 12, 2002.
Jeffrey Young	"Eradicating Afghanistan's Opium Poppies," *Voice of America*, June 24, 2005. www.voanews.com.

CHAPTER 4

What Is the Political Climate in Afghanistan?

Chapter Preface

Since the September 11, 2001, terrorist attacks, the U.S. government has made the spread of democracy, especially in the Muslim world, a top foreign policy priority. The first application of the policy has been the attempt to transform Afghanistan into a functioning democratic state. President George W. Bush has frequently stated that the establishment of democracies in the Muslim world is the only way to prevent future acts of terror. He has also insisted that Islam and democracy are not incompatible. "It should be clear to all that Islam, the faith of one-fifth of humanity, is consistent with democratic rule," Bush argues. "A religion that demands individual moral accountability and encourages the encounter of the individual with God is fully compatible with the rights and responsibilities of self-government." Despite his positive words, many analysts contend that trying to impose democracy on Afghanistan will fail.

Critics of the president's policy believe that the goal is both naive and unachievable. Paul M. Weyrich, chair of the Free Congress Foundation, asserts, "If the nations of the Middle East renounce Islam, then President Bush's vision will work. If they stick to a death-oriented religion where the greatest act one can perform is to kill Christians and Jews, then the ideals of pluralistic democracy and freedom will hardly prevail." Other commentators agree. "In the eyes of Islam," writes author Jamie Glazov, "the very notion of democracy is demonized. In Islam, after all, Allah [God] is sovereign, which means that humans constructing their own laws is sinful."

However, many voices within the Muslim world are calling out for democracy. For example, according to Fatma al Sayegh of United Arab Emirates University, "For a majority of Muslims, democracy does not seem to contradict Islam. On the contrary, Islam and democracy are compatible and complement each other in many ways. Most Muslims believe that democracy in no way threatens their religious values and societal freedom."

Indeed, democracies already exist in the Muslim world. The most prominent examples are Turkey and Indonesia. Turkey's brand of democracy differs in many ways from America's, however. Secularism is mandated—not just in the nation's institutions, but in individual behavior. For example, politicians are prohibited from making public displays of religion; women are not allowed to wear veils or headscarves in government buildings and schools; and citizens are discouraged from identifying themselves primarily by their religion. After decades of authoritarian rule, Indonesia is slowly transforming itself into a functioning democracy. Interestingly, both Indonesia and Turkey, while Muslim majority nations, are non-Arab, which suggests to some that the lack of democracy in the Middle East has more to do with Arab culture and traditions than the Islamic faith.

The transition from authoritarian rule to democracy is always difficult. Democracy is about more than just elections. For a democracy to succeed, it must build stable institutions that enshrine and defend liberty, equality, and human rights. Whether Afghanistan will evolve into a successful Islamic democracy by investing in democratic institutions will only be known decades from now.

> "Who among us could have imagined
> what the people of Afghanistan would
> achieve in this short time? A new,
> democratic constitution."

Afghanistan Is an Emerging Democracy

Condoleezza Rice

In the following viewpoint Condoleezza Rice argues that the Afghan people, with the help of the United States and its coalition partners, are creating the basic institutions necessary for democracy. A democratic constitution has been passed, and free elections have been held, Rice notes. Although the progress made since the ousting of the fundamentalist Muslim Taliban regime in 2001 is impressive, Rice notes, there is still work to do. In her view, Afghanistan's international partners must make a long-term commitment to ensure that the nation matures into a stable, prosperous democracy. Condoleezza Rice is U.S. secretary of state.

As you read, consider the following questions:

1. According to Rice, what is NATO's role in Afghanistan?

Condoleezza Rice, "Remarks at the Afghanistan Compact Meeting," http://www.state.gov/secretary/rm/2006/60098.htm, January 31, 2006. U.S. Department of State, Washington, D.C.

2. What was the result of the Taliban's rule, according to the author?

3. According to Rice, how will democracy in Afghanistan impact the Middle East?

What brings us together today is a monumental achievement of our young century: the ongoing transformation of Afghanistan from tyranny to democracy. This triumph is a credit, first and foremost, to the noble Afghan people, to the leadership of President [Hamid] Karzai, and it is, as such, an example of what the world can achieve when we all work together.

Ravaged and Ruined

We all remember the Afghanistan of the past. A country ravaged and ruined by the Taliban's cruelty. A country completely isolated from the world and home to [the terrorist group] al-Qaida. A country where human dignity was trampled, where liberty was deemed an impure thought, and where soccer stadiums became killing fields for women guilty only of learning to read.

After the United States and our allies removed the Taliban regime, the Afghan people set out to liberate themselves. They did so with the international community by their side. And today, we mark the fulfillment of the ambitious vision that we all set out together [in 2002] in Bonn, Germany: a fully functioning, sovereign Afghan government.

Who among us could have imagined what the people of Afghanistan would achieve in this short time? A new, democratic constitution. An emerging free economy. A growing, multi-ethnic army that is the pride of the Afghan people. Successful presidential and parliamentary elections in which millions of citizens—men and women—voted freely for the first time.

The international support for Afghanistan has been extensive and impressive. Many different countries are lending their

Bob Englehart. Reproduced by permission.

expertise and resources to reconstruction. Regional partners are joining together to help, along with the United Nations and the European Union. And many countries, like Japan and Great Britain, and of course Germany, have distinguished themselves through their overwhelming generosity and dedication.

On the security side, NATO [North Atlantic Treaty Organization] is leading the international effort to help the Afghan people secure their new democracy. Our hosts, the United Kingdom, are stepping up to lead this deployment, as it expands throughout Afghanistan. And our friends in Canada deserve special thanks for their essential contribution to this important NATO mission.

Long-Term Success

With so much progress, some could be tempted to think that the hard work is done. President Bush and I do not share this view. Nor do the American people. The United States is fully devoted to the long-term success of Afghanistan. For us, this is a strategic partnership. We have committed tens of thousands of our troops to help stabilize the country. We have sacrificed precious American lives. And now, in addition to our current commitment of nearly $6 billion, today, I am proud to announce that President Bush will ask our Congress for $1.1 billion in new assistance to support the Afghan people in [2006].

The [Bonn] Compact . . . sets out an inspiring vision for the future of Afghanistan—a future of liberty and tolerance, and permanent peace. Today, we renew the purpose of our multilateral partnership: to empower the Afghan people to guarantee democracy's enduring success—not just as a form of governance, but as a way of life.

To ensure the security of Afghan democracy, the country's army and police must be fully capable to act on their own, to protect the lives and liberties of their citizens, and to defeat the terrorists and militants who still threaten democracy's progress.

To ensure the prosperity of Afghan democracy, the country's economy must continue to offer greater opportunities for farmers, and traders, and entrepreneurs to succeed in the legal free market—without being driven into the underground economy or narcotics trade. And Afghanistan must again find its rightful place in the region's economy and economic development.

Finally, to ensure the integrity of Afghan democracy, the country's constitution, and the laws that its National Assembly will soon pass, must translate into an effective system of justice for all Afghans.

The transformation of Afghanistan is remarkable but, of course, still incomplete. And it is essential that we all increase our support for the Afghan people.

Patriots

In Afghanistan today, the world is witnessing an unprecedented moment in the history of freedom. The impatient patriots of Afghanistan are helping to lead the expansion of liberty throughout the Broader Middle East. They are affirming— just as Europeans, and Asians, and Africans, and indeed Americans themselves did at earlier times—that the longing for liberty and self-government is universally desired, and universally deserved.

This remarkable journey, which many thought impossible only [a few] years ago, will one day, in retrospect, seem to have been inevitable. So let us recommit ourselves, let us redouble our efforts, to the future of Afghanistan, knowing that in a safe and secure and democratic Afghanistan the world will have a lasting friend and a lasting fighter for peace. Let us achieve that future together.

| "*There is no prospect that even the semblance of a democratic regime will emerge in Afghanistan.*"

Afghanistan Is Not a Democracy

Mike Head

In the following viewpoint Mike Head argues that the new Afghan constitution enshrines reactionary Islamic theology and therefore cannot be considered democratic. He also claims that President Hamid Karzai is an American puppet who will act in the interests of America, not his fellow Afghans. Despite the fact that the George W. Bush administration and much of the media claim that Afghanistan has been successfully transformed from a brutal dictatorship into a democracy, much of the country is run by drug lords and their private armies, he maintains. Mike Head is a news analyst for the World Socialist Web Site.

As you read, consider the following questions:

1. According to the author, who were the majority of the delegates to the 2004 grand tribal council in Afghanistan?

Mike Head, "US-imposed 'Democracy' in Afghanistan," World Socialist Web Site, January 8, 2004. Reproduced by permission.

2. What happened after a female social worker complained about the membership of the grand tribal council, according to Head?

3. In Head's view, why is Afghanistan likely to become a military dictatorship?

After more than three weeks of cajoling, back-room haggling and standover tactics, the 502 largely unelected delegates to the United States-orchestrated *loya jirga*, or grand tribal council, in Afghanistan endorsed a constitution aimed at strengthening the crumbling position of Washington's hand-picked interim president, Hamid Karzai.

Following intense arm-twisting of faction leaders by US President George Bush's envoy and ambassador to Afghanistan, Zalmay Khalilzad, and UN [United Nations] special envoy Lakhdar Brahimi, the assembly—a huge tent full of representatives of warlords, mullahs and outright US stooges—rubber-stamped a constitution on January 4 [2004].

A Travesty

While media reports presented the outcome as a triumph for democracy, the assembly was a travesty from start to finish. Karzai selected 50 of the delegates, while the various militia, religious and ethnic elites that have been complicit in the US-led military occupation, chose the others. Amid growing resistance to the puppet regime, they could only meet under armed guard. Even then, the proceedings were threatened by a series of rocket attacks on the site.

Perhaps the most revealing moment came when Malalai Joya, a 26-year-old female social worker from the rural province of Farah, stood up to condemn most of the jirga's committee chairmen as criminals. Instead of being given influential positions, she declared, they should be tried for their crimes. Joya was initially thrown out of the meeting, then allowed to remain and is now under UN protection from death threats.

The crimes to which she referred were the widespread rocket shellings, torture, rape and mass killings of civilians committed by Islamic fundamentalist warlords—mujahideen, or holy warriors—from 1992 to 1996 before they were ousted by the Taliban extremists. The US and its allies are today relying upon the same thugs to rule Afghanistan. One of the most prominent delegates was General Abdul Rashid Dostum, whose Northern Alliance forces massacred thousands of Taliban prisoners in the desert near Mazar-i-Sharif during the US invasion in November 2001.

An Anti-Democratic Process

So anti-democratic was the entire process that no vote was even taken on the final version of the document. Instead, at the urging of the chairman, most of those present simply stood briefly to signify their acceptance. Just three days earlier, the meeting had been suspended in disarray when some 40 percent of the delegates boycotted the first and only vote at the gathering.

Led by former president Burhanuddin Rabbani, the coalition of minority ethnic factions, including his Tajik clan, Uzbeks and Hazaras, called for the appointment of a prime minister to restrict the sweeping powers allocated to the president. They also demanded official recognition of minority languages and called for a ban on ministers holding dual citizenship. The latter provision was primarily directed at those in Karzai's camp who are US citizens.

An Autocratic Presidency

Once Khalilzad and Brahimi stepped in to lay down the law, Rabbani and his allies quickly acceded to an autocratic presidency. The president will rule without a prime minister. He will have the power to appoint and dismiss ministers, key officials, judges and military, police and intelligence chiefs, as well as one-third of the upper house of the national assembly. He will be the commander-in-chief of the armed forces and can declare states of emergency for the whole or parts of the country.

In return, Karzai and his backers made minor concessions. They added a second vice president to represent minority interests and gave the national assembly the right to approve some presidential appointments. Alongside the two official languages, Pashto (spoken by ethnic Pashtuns) and Dari (Tajik), other languages will be recognised in regions where they are spoken by a majority of people. Apparently, Karzai agreed to learn Uzbek. There will be no ban on dual citizenship, but the national assembly can reject individual officials who hold foreign passports.

Lip Service

Karzai also struck a deal with hard-line Islamic fundamentalists to include a clause prohibiting any law from offending Islam. This means that, despite the lip service paid by the constitution to democratic rights, including equal status for women, reactionary Islamic precepts will prevail. Karzai had already appointed Fazal Hadi Shinwari as chief justice of the Supreme Court. In violation of the constitution, Shinwari is over the age limit and has training only in religious, not secular, law.

He is an ally of the pro-Wahhabi, Saudi-backed fundamentalist leader Ustad Abdul Rasul Sayyaf, who was a committee chairman in the *loya jirga*. Shinwari has packed the Supreme Court with sympathetic mullahs, called for Taliban-style punishments and brought back the Taliban's dreaded Ministry for the Promotion of Virtue and Prevention of Vice, renamed the Ministry of Haj and Religious Affairs. It deploys squads to stop public displays of "un-Islamic" behaviour among Afghan women.

Presidential elections are meant to be held under the new constitution by June [2004, but was not held until December,]

Another Taliban

The new Afghanistan Constitution represents at least a temporary improvement over the tyrannical rule of the Taliban, but it will not establish a truly free country, only the veneer of a free country. By enshrining Islam as a political force, the new Constitution has laid the groundwork for another Taliban.

Allen Forkum, Capitalism Magazine, *January 15, 2004.*

to be followed by assembly elections. But the deteriorating economic and security situation in the country makes that schedule unlikely. UN envoy Brahimi has already told the *New York Times* that assembly elections would be "well nigh impossible" because the threat of Taliban insurgents make large parts of the country inaccessible. [Presidential and assembly elections have been since held.]

For his part, Rabbani has made it plain that the conflicts that wracked the *loya jirga* have by no means receded. He declared that the backroom dictates issued in Kabul had only damaged the administration's credibility and warned that the strong presidential system could "push Afghanistan to a dictatorship".

U.S. Military Control

Despite the deeply reactionary character of the gathering in Kabul, UN secretary-general Kofi Annan praised the outcome as an historic achievement. President Bush welcomed the constitution, declaring that "a democratic Afghanistan will serve the interests and just aspirations of all the Afghan people".

The major media outlets, including the erstwhile liberal press, dutifully echoed these remarks. The *New York Times* editorial called the constitution "enlightened" and said the

Bush administration was "justifiably thrilled by the outcome". It endorsed ongoing US military control of the country, "to help provide the political support and military security to make presidential and parliamentary elections possible".

To even speak of democracy in these circumstances is farcical. Washington has illegally conquered one of the most impoverished and ruined countries on earth, overturned its government and joined hands with notorious butchers to repress and intimidate the population. Around 12,000 US-led combat troops remain in Afghanistan, terrorising the population in the name of hunting down Taliban and Al Qaeda [terrorist group] supporters. They are accompanied by 5,700 NATO [North Atlantic Treaty Organisation] "peacekeepers," which are mainly propping up the Karzai administration in the capital.

Even the timetable for elections in Afghanistan is driven by the Bush administration's immediate domestic political considerations. It badly needs a symbolic show of success for its "war on terror" in the lead-up to the US presidential election in November [2004]. It is proceeding with its characteristic mixture of cynicism and short-sightedness. All that matters in Afghanistan is a public relations victory, regardless of the completely catastrophic reality.

Deteriorating Security

Many parts of the country are no longer safe for allied troops, or for that matter, UN officials, aid workers and ordinary civilians. Mounting guerilla attacks have forced international aid agencies to withdraw to Kabul, halting even elementary welfare efforts. On December 18 [2003], the World Food Program admitted that its food distribution program had been severely affected by the breakdown in security.

The deteriorating situation was highlighted on January 6 [2004], when a truck-bomb blast near a military base in the southern city of Kandahar killed at least 16 people and wounded 52, many of them school children. Despite the indiscriminate terror employed by the insurgents, the methods being employed by the US seem to be simply increasing support for the Taliban fundamentalists.

Heavy-handed repression by US troops is intensifying popular opposition and resistance to the occupation, particularly in the southern and eastern Pashtun regions. [In December 2003], the US military launched its largest operations in Afghanistan since the overthrow of the Taliban, aimed at tracking down anti-government forces and quelling wider unrest in the lead-up to the *loya jirga*.

Drug Barons and Private Armies

Karzai's fiefdom is largely confined to Kabul, where US troops guard him around the clock. Elsewhere, private armies roam, with a total of half a million men under arms, some linked to drug barons and others to members of Karzai's government.

There is no prospect that even the semblance of a democratic regime will emerge in Afghanistan under these hellish and neo-colonial conditions. Democracy is only possible through a genuine popular revolution, spearheaded by the working class, throughout the Middle East and Central Asia. Only such a movement could liberate the region from decades of great power domination and overcome its legacy of economic backwardness, warlordism and theocratic oppression.

> "The people of Afghanistan have made great strides towards peace, stability, and democracy."

Afghanistan Is Becoming Stable

Hamid Karzai

According to Afghan president Hamid Karzai in the following viewpoint, Afghanistan has made great progress since the overthrow of the Taliban regime and is on the road to becoming a stable, prosperous democracy. He contends that continued international assistance in battling the illegal narcotics trade, building democratic institutions, and strengthening security have been essential in stabilizing Afghanistan. The Afghan people are grateful to the many nations of the world that have contributed militarily and economically to the rebirth of their country, he asserts.

As you read, consider the following questions:

1. According to Karzai, what are Afghanistan's two most serious challenges?
2. What areas of Afghanistan's infrastructure need special attention, according to the author?

Hamid Karzai, "Remarks Delivered at The London Conference on Afghanistan," http://www.foc.gov.uk/servlet/front?pagename=openmarket/xcelerate/showpage&c=page&cid=0036906260508&a=karticle&aid=1136909634037, January 31, 2006. Reproduced by permission.

3. According to the author, how has the status of women improved in Afghanistan?

The people of Afghanistan have made great strides towards peace, stability and democracy. We owe our successes to the resilience and unfailing determination of the Afghan people as well as the generous support of the international community. Together we have achieved much. Today Afghanistan has a constitution, an elected President and an elected Parliament. We are proud that women make up more than a quarter of the seats in our National Assembly. Where four years ago [in 2002], education was in a state of total collapse, today more than six million girls and boys are attending schools. Our national economy is growing steadily and, over the past four years, we have enjoyed a total real GDP [gross domestic product] growth of 85 percent, while the rate of inflation has been kept at around 10 percent.

We have taken major steps to reconstitute our military and police forces. Whereas four years ago Afghanistan was a haven for international terrorism, today our country is a full participant in the global fight against terrorism. Four years ago, the Bonn Agreement presented us with a formidable set of objectives. Today, I am pleased that we successfully conclude the Bonn Process and open a new chapter of Afghanistan's rebuilding and partnership with the international community.

A Long Road Ahead

However, in spite of the achievements, we have a long road ahead and significant challenges still to meet. We have re-established our institutions of governance and justice, but these need to develop to serve the interests of the Afghan people.

Our resurgent economy will need many more years to grow at substantial levels before it can uplift the majority of our people from poverty.

And above all challenges, terrorism and narcotics represent the gravest of threats. Terrorism no longer rules Afghanistan, but it continues to be a threat to our people's security and welfare. It is not the security and independence of Afghanistan alone that is threatened by terrorism; this menace is the enemy of peace and of humanity, and is responsible for the massacre of innocent people across the world. Any weakness in our resolve to fight terrorism will only embolden it and result in greater human loss.

The threat of narcotics must be fought through law enforcement and through alternative economic opportunities. This fight will prove arduous and unremitting. In the past year [2005] we reduced the land under poppy cultivation by 21%, mainly through voluntary self-restraint, and we are determined to take further steps to completely eliminate this menace. We expect the international community to co-operate with us realistically, not only to help us root out narcotics, but to do so without causing undue economic hardship and instability.

To overcome the challenges that remain in the security, economic and state-building, Afghanistan has prepared a national development strategy. . . .

Through this strategy, and with continued assistance from the international community, we will work to address the priorities that we have set ourselves over the next five years.

Building Institutions

We understand that lasting peace and security in Afghanistan will ultimately depend on building effective and capable institutions of governance. Through developing institutional capacities of the state, we will enforce the rule of law and ensure the protection of the rights of our people. We will expedite administrative and judicial reforms, remove red-tape, create an efficient and transparent administration, and fight corruption and nepotism. Building a modern state capable of deliv-

Improving Security and Stability

Security and stability are improving as the new Afghan National Army (ANA) and the Afghan National Police grow in size. The central government is gradually but surely extending its authority throughout the country.... Twelve ANA battalions consisting of 6,000 troops have been trained and are on full-time duty, with a goal of 10,000 by June 2004 and 70,000 eventually. The ANA is a disciplined fighting force capable of conducting both combat and civil-military-affairs, and is currently helping coalition forces hunt down remnants of the Taliban regime.

White House press release, January 22, 2004.

ering services to its people is dependent upon a skilled and educated workforce.

We request the international community to pay special attention to assistance to the development of our human capital.

To improve our economy, we will focus on strengthening our country's infrastructure with particular focus on energy—especially electricity, road networks and water. We will create an enabling environment for business to grow and for our farmers to produce and market. We aim to expand our domestic revenue base, focusing on customs, mining, utilizing state assets and other sources of growth. While seeking international aid to rebuild our economic infrastructure and provide for our energy needs, we will encourage foreign direct investment and private sector investors to seize opportunities available in Afghanistan.

We will also promote our macro-economic stability by seeking debt-relief from our international creditors through the Paris Club arrangement.

Improving Security

On the security front, fighting terrorism, in close conjunction with the active military presence in Afghanistan of the international community is our priority. We are pleased with the expansion of NATO [North Atlantic Treaty Organization] forces in Afghanistan, and hope their role will be consistent with the demands of security and stability in Afghanistan. We hope you will continue and increase your support in equipping and training our national army, police and other security forces. The size, quality and mobility of our military and security forces must be raised in proportion to the level of the challenge faced by our country.

We will also consolidate the success of our disarmament, demobilization and reintegrating programme by continuing the disarmament of illegal armed groups that are still present in Afghanistan.

To support the implementation of our national development strategy, we are pleased that the international community is joining us in the Afghanistan Compact today. Through the Compact, we the people of Afghanistan renew our pledge to build on the successes of the Bonn Process and lead our nation's economic, social and political development. The international community and Afghanistan are mutually committed to meeting the benchmarks set out in the Compact.

As we strengthen our capacity to deliver services and manage our development process, we expect the international community to provide a greater portion of its contribution to the Afghan Government.

The government of Afghanistan is fully committed to reach the goals of the Compact by implementing the ANDS [Afghan National Development Strategy]. We thank the international community for its confidence and continued support. I wish to thank the United Nations for their active role in our political development and state-building efforts, Germany for being host of the 2001 Bonn and the 2004 Berlin conferences, and

Japan for hosting the 2002 Tokyo Conference. I also thank each and every nation and organization . . . that has supported Afghanistan in so many ways.

A Grateful Nation

You have given so generously, and your assistance has given strength and renewed resolve to our people; your soldiers are bringing security to our homes. As a nation, we are grateful for what you have done for us.

I take this opportunity to remember your soldiers and workers who laid down their precious lives, alongside the Afghans, while serving Afghanistan. The Afghan people honour their memory.

Today the people of Afghanistan are proud that, with your help, we have been able to regain our place in the family of nations as an integral and dignified member. A stable, peaceful and prosperous Afghanistan is not a blessing for the Afghans alone; it is for all of us.

On behalf of the Afghan people, I pledge today that we will be a dependable asset to the security of the region and of the world.

| "Far from creating the conditions for stability to evolve in Afghanistan, US policy is having the opposite effect."

Afghanistan Is Unstable

Meena Nanji

Meena Nanji argues in the following viewpoint that Afghanistan's new undemocratic constitution was created by warlords and fundamentalists, who terrorize the populace. There are no legitimate political parties, and voters—especially women—are intimidated by extremists. Afghanistan is rapidly becoming a lawless narcostate as well, Nanji maintains. Meena Nanji is an ethnic South Asian and an independent filmmaker living in Los Angeles.

As you read, consider the following questions:

1. According to Nanji, how was Afghanistan's constitution ratified?

2. How is the United States supporting warlords, in the author's opinion?

3. According to the author, what are conditions like for women in Afghanistan?

Meena Nanji, "Democracy in Afghanistan?" *Z Magazine*, February 23, 2004. Reproduced by permission of the author.

With Iraq an unmitigated disaster . . . , U.S President George Bush desperately needs a success story in his foreign policy pursuits to justify the unleashing of the U.S's gargantuan military might against impoverished nations. What better way than to trumpet the triumph of "democracy"—that sacrosanct term that opens the hearts of ordinary Americans eager to believe that their government is doing "Right" in the world. With plans for Iraq's installation of "democracy" proving far too popular with the "wrong" kind of people for Washington's tastes, Afghanistan seems to be once again cast to serve the Bush administration's needs, this time by being paraded as the grateful—and successful—recipient of US-exported "democracy.". . .

Rosy Rhetoric

Bush's rosy rhetoric about Afghanistan has already been stepped up. In his [2004] State of the Union address he said:

"As of this month, that country has a new constitution, guaranteeing free elections and full participation by women. . . . With help from the new Afghan army, our coalition is leading aggressive raids against the surviving members of the Taliban and [the terrorist group] Al Qaeda. The men and women of Afghanistan are building a nation that is free and proud and fighting terror."

Yet, as in the case of Iraq, it seems that the president is again suffering from faulty intelligence. His remarks seem to bear little resemblance to the reality that is Afghanistan today and certainly merit closer scrutiny.

Anything but Democratic

True, Afghanistan does have a new constitution, ratified on January 4, 2004. However, it was a product of dubious means: The Loya Jirga, or Grand Assembly, in which the constitution was meant to be debated was dominated by fundamentalist mujahideen [religious warriors] and warlords who did not in-

A Deteriorating Situation

On the security front, situation is fast deteriorating. Pakistan is back at its old game of causing instability through the Inter-Services Intelligence. The regrouping of the Taliban and al-Qaeda along the Pakistan-Afghanistan border and the increasing intensity of trans-border clashes exemplify this. Media and other inputs point to close coordination and orchestration by jihadi groups led by the Jaish-e-Mohammad and operating out of *madrassas* (religious schools) in Quetta and North-West Frontier Province in Pakistan.

Arun Sahgal, Asia Times, *September 4, 2003*

spire open discussion. International human rights groups and local Afghan journalists reported that decisions were "agreed upon" not through free and equal participation but by physical intimidation of delegates, vote-buying, death threats and backroom decisions between government officials and influential militia leaders that excluded a majority of delegates. In short the "ratification" of the constitution was anything but democratic.

The constitution itself also has many problems. While on paper it does make sweeping enunciations of equality, democracy, economic, civil and political rights, there is little about creating the institutions to uphold or implement these provisions. Without the means to actually enforce laws, the constitution carries little authority—perhaps none in the face of armed warlords. How it can "guarantee free elections" is therefore something of a mystery.

Supporting the Warlords

Meanwhile, the US claims it is supporting peace and democracy in Afghanistan. For the last two years [2002–2004], the

US has embarked on operation after operation to "root out" remnants of the Taliban and Al Qaeda in its "war on terror". While this in itself may not be cause for concern, what is alarming are the tactics and policies employed by the US in doing so. Indeed, far from creating the conditions for stability to evolve in Afghanistan, US policy is having the opposite effect. Much of the violence that is raging throughout the country is arguably a direct result of US policies:

a) The US's most egregious policy is the forging of unholy alliances between the US military and known war criminals. Far from getting "help from the new Afghan army," (which consists of a paltry 7000 men, rather short of its aim of 70,000, and already suffering hundreds of desertions), the US is relying on regional warlords and their militias for support in pursuing the Taliban. It seems not to matter to the US that the differences in outlook between the Taliban and these warlords is minimal: most are as dictatorial, fundamentalist, and anti-modern as the Taliban. They are also the same people who dominated Afghanistan during its chaotic civil war era from 1992–96. The Taliban did succeed in disarming these warlords and restoring some kind of order to the country.

Thus when Taliban rule ended, there was a real opportunity for the creation of a strong government without the dominance of armed warlords to contest its authority. However, the U.S chose to resurrect the warlords by supporting them once again with cash and arms.

b) The U.S has until very recently opposed the expansion of international peacekeepers to the rest of the country. The International Security Assistance Forces (ISAF) is undoubtedly the reason for relative peace and stability in Kabul. With their presence, the power of private armies loyal to highly placed ministers, such as Defense Minister General Fahim, has been diffused; commercial activity has been allowed to progress, aid workers can work openly, women have been able to take part in public and civic life with relative safety. NATO [North Atlantic Treaty Organization] decided last October [2003] to expand their forces, although so far significant numbers of troops have not been forthcoming. The US is now pushing for NATO to deploy provincial reconstruction teams, or PRT's. PRT's are not designated peacekeepers but do humanitarian work, such as build schools here and there. They have little impact on security, and have no power to intervene in factional fighting or in human rights abuses perpetrated by militia.

c) Disarmament of the estimated 100,000–500,000 armed men in Afghanistan has also been moving at an extremely slow pace even though it is considered by most Afghans to be the first and most vital step toward the rule of law and away from the gun. Indeed the US is further undermining disarmament by re-arming regional warlords in the name of fighting terror.

Taken together, these policies have allowed the warlords to once again consolidate their regional domination, which they are using to terrorize their citizenry with extortion, rape and killings. There is no talk of their being held accountable for their past and present crimes.

A Narco-State

The re-emergence of warlords has also resulted in another fateful development: Afghanistan is again the foremost opium producer in the world, producing an estimated nine times the amount of opium now than it did under Taliban rule. Recently, the U.N warned that Afghanistan is on the brink of becoming a narco-state where drug barons will be more powerful than the government. . . .

Already, many Afghans do not take this sudden appearance of "democracy" all too seriously, believing that it is the product of self-serving interests of the powers that be. Real democracy, they say, is impossible until the powerful warlords have been disarmed. Exclusion [from democratic processes] would also exacerbate ethnic tensions, further destabilizing the country. . . .

Women Continue to Suffer

Only a handful of women have benefited from increased opportunities in vocations and education and they are largely restricted to Kabul. The ratification of The Convention on the Elimination of All Forms of Discrimination against Women (CEDAW) in March 2003 has had no effect on the well-being of Afghan women, and there is little reason to expect that their stated "equality" in the Constitution will have any positive effect either. The vast majority of Afghan women remain illiterate and uneducated and under oppressive traditions. Militiamen target them for rape, torture and kidnapping. Girls' schools are being set on fire. Laws are being upheld that restrict women's education and public appearances. Many women cannot receive health care either because clinics are too dangerous to get to, or because male doctors can't treat them. Though illegal, forced and under-age marriages are still common. In Herat, a new phenomenon has emerged . . . , that of self-immolation: women are so desperate and fearful of men that they actually set themselves on fire.

Under these circumstances it is wholly disingenuous of Bush to claim "free elections and the full participation by women", especially in the face of the insecurity that his administration has helped to promote. The Bush administration has done very little to ensure better conditions for women. If anything, it has done more to ensure their continued enslavement by supporting fundamentalists within and outside of government who are notorious for their brutal treatment of women and flagrant human rights violations. . . .

George Bush is confirming his own penchant for the appearance of democracy rather than any real participation in the political process by a majority of citizenry. But then, what kind of "democracy" can we expect when it is "exported" by a President who himself was installed by a backroom decision that overrode the popular vote?

Periodical Bibliography

The following articles have been selected to supplement the diverse views presented in this chapter.

John Barry	"Afghanistan: New Proposals for How the U.S. Can Help: Plans for Increasing Security in an Unstable Land," *Newsweek*, August 5, 2002.
Robert Charles	"The Afghan Dilemma," *Washington Times*, April 26, 2005.
Fred E. Foldvary	"Democracy for Afghanistan," *Progress Report*, December 2001.
Carlotta Gall	"In Afghanistan, Violence Stalls Renewal Effort," *New York Times*, April 26, 2003.
Sonali Kolhatkar and Jim Ingalls	"Giving Democracy a Bad Name," *Z Magazine*, September 16, 2005.
Jim Lobe	"Ugly Elections," *New Internationalist*, September 2004.
Robert M. Perito	Testimony before the Senate Foreign Relations Committee, May 12, 2004. www.foreign.senate.gov.
Ken Sanders	"On the Brink of Complete Strategic Failure in Afghanistan," *Dissident Voice*, May 25, 2005.
M. Nazif Shahrani	"Afghanistan's Presidential Elections: Spreading Democracy or a Sham?" *Middle East Report Online*, October 8, 2004. www.merip.org.
Peter Symonds	"Afghanistan's Presidential Election: A Mockery of Democracy," World Socialist Web Site, October 2, 2004. www.wsws.org.
Peter Willems	"Power Struggle Goes On: Security in Afghanistan Is Coming Apart," *Middle East*, August/September 2004.

For Further Discussion

Chapter 1

1. Mary Matalin argues that American successes in Afghanistan are not being reported by the mainstream media. From your experience, do you agree or disagree? Explain your answer.

2. According to Peter Symonds, claims that Afghanistan is a fledgling democracy are false. What evidence does he adduce to support his claims? Are his arguments compelling? Why or why not?

3. Austin Bay contends that successful elections in Afghanistan demonstrate the first success in the global war on terrorism. Do you agree or disagree? Explain.

Chapter 2

1. Laura Bush claims that Afghan women have made great progress since the overthrow of the Taliban, particularly in education. The Revolutionary Alliance of the Women of Afghanistan (RAWA), however, says women are now worse off under the Northern Alliance, and have no access to education. What aspects of Bush's and RAWA's arguments do you agree with? Which do you disagree with? Why?

2. Nazir Gul contends that women in Afghanistan are worse off today than they were under the Taliban. Do you believe mistreatment of women is a characteristic shared by most Muslim nations, or is Afghanistan a special case? Explain.

Chapter 3

1. Robert B. Scheer claims that U.S. efforts to eliminate poppy cultivation in Afghanistan have failed. Is his argument convincing? Why or why not?

2. Vanda Felbab-Brown believes that Afghanistan should be licensed to produce legal painkillers for medicinal use. Do you think this would be a good solution to Afghanistan's drug problem? Why or why not? Describe some other possible solutions to the problem of the illegal drug trade in Afghanistan.

Chapter 4

1. Condoleezza Rice argues that Afghanistan has made great progress toward becoming a modern democratic state, but Mike Head contends that the Afghan president is an American puppet trying to manage an emerging Islamic theocracy. Whose argument is more convincing? Explain.

2. Afghan president Hamid Karzai asserts that his nation is making great strides but that continued international involvement is still necessary. Do you believe the United States and other donor nations should remain involved in Afghanistan? Why or why not? If you agree with Karzai, for how long should the United States and other nations be involved? Explain your answer.

Organizations to Contact

Afghanistan Foundation
209 Pennsylvania Ave. SE, Suite 700, Washington, DC   20003
(202) 543-1177
e-mail: info@afghanistanfoundation.org
Web site: www.afghanistanfoundation.org

The Afghanistan Foundation was set up in 1996 as a partnership between Americans and Afghans designed to bring peace, stability, and prosperity to Afghanistan and to reduce confrontation in Central and South Asia. To further these objectives, the foundation has a number of projects, including the Afghanistan Charter Project, which brings together Afghan scholars and leaders from around the world to discuss how to establish a democratic government in Afghanistan. In another major project, a senior task force, which includes U.S. senators and Afghan government officials, was set up to make recommendations on U.S. policy toward Afghanistan. The full text of their report is available on the foundation's Web site.

Afghanistan Relief Organization (ARO)
PO Box 10207, Canoga Park, CA   91304
(818) 709-7011
Web site: www.afghanrelief.org

ARO was established in 1997 in response to the economic and physical hardships suffered by the Afghan people after decades of war. It is a volunteer organization funded by public donations and takes clothing, blankets, tents, and hygiene and other relief supplies to the poorest people in Afghanistan. The organization collects donations from American schools under its School Supply Project, which is designed to help educate Afghan youth who have lived their whole lives in wars and violent conflicts. The organization provides information on how to contact Afghan Americans for interviews or help with research on Afghanistan.

Afghanistan Research and Evaluation Unit (AREU)
Charahi Ansari, Kabul
  Afghanistan
(882) 168-980-0144
e-mail: areu@areu.org.af
Web site: www.areu.org.af

AREU is an independent organization that conducts action-oriented research to assist in formulation of government policies for reconstruction and development in Afghanistan. AREU was established by the international aid community in 2002, and has representatives from the United Nations and government and nongovernment organizations on its advisory board. Its Web site features a number of publications, including *A Guide to Government in Afghanistan.*

American Enterprise Institute for
Public Policy Research (AEI)
1150 Seventeenth St. NW, Washington, DC   20036
(202) 862-5800
Web site: www.aei.org

AEI is a conservative research and education organization that studies national and international issues, including American foreign policy. It promotes the spread of democracy and believes the United States should continue to be a world leader. Among its many activities, AEI hosts conferences in Washington, D.C., to bring together scholars and government officials to discuss U.S. policy in Afghanistan. Papers from these conferences are available on its Web site as well as the latest news and commentary on Afghanistan. AEI publishes the monthlies *American Enterprise* and *AEI Economist*, the bimonthly *Public Opinion*, and various books on America's foreign policy.

American Fund for Afghan Children (AFAC)
c/o The White House, Washington, DC   20509-1600
Web site: www.redcross.org

In October 2001 President George W. Bush announced the creation of America's Fund for Afghan Children in response to the concern expressed by Americans for the plight of the children in war-torn Afghanistan. In order to help provide food, shelter, education, and health care for Afghan children, the president asked that each American child contribute one dollar to the fund. AFAC funds are administered by the American Red Cross, which reports on the fund's activities on its Web site.

CARE
151 Ellis St. NE, Atlanta, GA   30303-2439
(800) 521-2273, ext. 999
Web site: www.care.org

As one of the world's largest international relief and development organizations, CARE reaches more than 35 million people in more than sixty developing nations in Africa, Asia, Latin America, and Europe. CARE works to provide basic education and immunization for children, economic and social empowerment for women, a stable supply of food and clean water, basic health care, and access to family planning services. CARE publishes an annual report and special reports on individual countries. Special reports on current events and CARE programs in Afghanistan are available on its Web site.

Cato Institute
1000 Massachusetts Ave. NW, Washington, DC   20001-5403
(202) 842-0200
e-mail: cato@cato.org
Web site: www.cato.org

The institute is a libertarian public policy research foundation dedicated to stimulating foreign policy debate. It publishes the *Cato Journal* three times a year, the periodic *Cato Policy Analysis*, and a bimonthly newsletter *Cato Policy Review*. Cato's Web site on terrorism includes articles on Afghanistan, the war on drugs, and recommendations for U.S. policies in Central and South Asia.

Center for Afghanistan Studies (CAS)
University of Nebraska–Omaha, Omaha, NE   68182
(402) 554-2800
Web site: www.unomaha.edu/world/cas

Established in 1972 at the University of Nebraska–Omaha, the CAS provides scholarly exchanges, technical assistance, and training to educational institutions in Afghanistan. With its field office in Kabul, CAS acts as a focal point for gathering together significant source materials and for contacts between Afghan specialists from around the world. The center offers various publications on its Web site, including a Dari/English dictionary.

EurasiaNet.Org
e-mail: info@eurasianet.org
Web site: www.eurasianet.org

EurasiaNet.org provides information and analysis of political, economic, environmental, and social developments in Russia and countries in Central Asia, the Caucasus, the Middle East, and Southwest Asia. The organization publishes an online journal, *Eurasia Insight,* which includes articles designed to inform policy makers in the United States and in the targeted regions on current events.

Help the Afghan Children International (HTACI)
8603 Westwood Center Dr., Suite 230, Vienna, VA   22182
(888) 403-0407
Web site: www.helptheafghanchildren.org

In 1993 Afghan American Suraya Sadeed established HTACI, a nonprofit organization designed to help Afghan women and children. The organization funds primary healthcare clinics, educational and vocational training projects, and innovative programs on peace education and environmental awareness. HTACI's publications include the *Voice of Innocence Newsletter,* which describes the organization's activities and includes articles on the latest developments in Afghanistan.

Human Rights Watch (HRW)
350 Fifth Ave., 34th Floor, New York, NY   10118-3299
(212) 290-4700
e-mail: hrwnyc@hrw.org
Web site: www.hrw.org

HRW is the largest human rights organization in the United States. With offices in New York; Washington, D.C.; Los Angeles; San Francisco; Brussels; London; and Geneva, HRW staff research and conduct fact-finding missions into human rights abuses in more than seventy countries. In July 2003 the organization published a controversial article, "Killing You Is a Very Easy Thing for Us to Do," about the continued human rights abuses in Afghanistan after the fall of the Taliban. Its publication *World Development Report 2004: Human Rights and Armed Conflicts* includes essays on Afghanistan.

Institute for Afghan Studies (IAS)
Web site: www.institute-for-afghan-studies.org

An online organization founded and operated by Afghan scholars from around the world, the goal of IAS is to promote a better understanding of Afghan affairs through scholarly research and studies. The IAS Web site gives information on the history and politics of Afghanistan and biographical information on key Afghan and Taliban leaders.

Islamic Republic of Afghanistan
Web site: www.af/

This central Web site of the government of the Islamic Republic of Afghanistan includes budget information, a donors database, links to government ministries, development plans, and speeches by government officials.

Revolutionary Association of the Women of Afghanistan (RAWA)
PO Box 374, Quetta
  Pakistan

(0092) (300) 855-1638
e-mail: rawa@rawa.org
Web site: www.rawa.org

Established in 1977 in Kabul, RAWA is an organization of Afghan women who are dedicated to peace, freedom, democracy, human rights, and social justice. The organization solicits public donations for relief aid and for projects to assist schools, orphanages, and women's cooperatives. RAWA's Web site includes press reports and journal articles on political, economic, and social issues in Afghanistan. Its recent publications include Anne Brodsky's *With All Our Strength: The Revolutionary Association of the Women of Afghanistan*, and Melody Ermachild Chavis's *Meena: Heroine of Afghanistan: The Martyr Who Founded RAWA.*

United Nations Assistance Mission to Afghanistan (UNAMA)
PO Box 5858, Grand Central Station
  New York, NY   10163-5858
e-mail: spokesman-unama@un.org
Web site: www.unama-afg.org

In 2002 the United Nations Security Council established UNAMA to integrate the activities of the sixteen UN agencies in Afghanistan. UNAMA's mandate includes promoting national reconciliation and human rights, and managing humanitarian relief projects. UNAMA has its head office in Kabul and has regional offices in the major provinces. Key UN documents and speeches by UN personnel on Afghanistan can be found on its Web site.

United States-Afghan Women's Council
fax: (202) 312-9663
e-mail: Hovanecsc@state.gov
Web site: http://usawc.state.gov

In February 2002 President George W. Bush and Afghan president Hamid Karzai announced the creation of the U.S.-Afghan Women's Council to promote cooperative ventures between women in their two countries to help Afghan women gain an education and find employment. The council is cochaired by the U.S. undersecretary for global affairs and the Afghan ministers of women's affairs and foreign affairs, and is staffed by the U.S. Department of State Office of International Women's Issues. Its Web site includes information on council projects as well as speeches and press releases on Afghan women's issues.

**United States Agency for
International Development (USAID)**
Ronald Reagan Bldg., Washington, DC   20523-0016
(202) 712-4810
Web site: www.usaid.gov

USAID is the U.S. government agency that implements America's foreign economic and humanitarian assistance programs and provides assistance to countries recovering from disaster, trying to escape poverty, and engaging in democratic reforms. USAID is an independent federal agency that receives overall foreign policy guidance from the secretary of state. The agency provides information on its policies and programs in Afghanistan on its Web site.

United States Department of State
Office of Public Communications, Washington, DC   20520
(202) 647-6575
e-mail: secretary@state.gov
Web site: www.state.gov

The Department of State advises the president in the formulation and execution of foreign policy, and includes the Bureau for International Narcotics and Law Enforcement Affairs, and the U.S. Counterterrorism Office, both of which manage programs in Afghanistan. Information on these programs as well as speeches by government officials are available on the department's Web site.

World Bank
1818 H St. NW, Washington, DC   20433
(202) 477-1234
Web site: www.worldbank.org

The World Bank is the world's largest source of development assistance funds, providing more than $18 billion in loans to its client countries in 2003–2004. The bank uses its financial resources and extensive knowledge base to help developing countries move to a path of stable, sustainable, and equitable growth. The organization publishes books and reports, including *The World Development Report*, which gives a global perspective on the developing world, and individual country studies, including studies on Afghanistan's economic performance and prospects. A special section on the bank's Web site features policy papers on Afghanistan, and provides information on World Bank projects in Afghanistan in the agriculture, health, education, and economic sectors.

Bibliography of Books

Jon Lee Anderson *The Lion's Grave: Dispatches from Afghanistan.* New York: Grove/ Atlantic, 2002.

Sally Armstrong *Veiled Threat: The Hidden Power of the Women of Afghanistan.* New York: Four Walls Eight Windows, 2003.

Adam Bennett *Reconstructing Afghanistan.* Washington: International Monetary Fund, 2005.

Anne Brodsky *With All Our Strength: The Revolutionary Association of the Women of Afghanistan.* New York: Routledge, 2003.

Melody Ermachild Chavis *Meena, Heroine of Afghanistan: The Martyr Who Founded RAWA, the Revolutionary Association of the Women of Afghanistan.* New York: St. Martin's, 2003.

Steve Coll *Ghost Wars: The Secret History of the CIA, Afghanistan, and Bin Laden, from the Soviet Invasion to September 10, 2001.* New York: Penguin, 2005.

Hafizullah Emadi *Repression, Resistance, and Women in Afghanistan.* Westport, CT: Praeger, 2002.

Martin Ewans *Afghanistan: A Short History of Its People and Politics.* New York: HarperCollins, 2002.

John Follain and Rita Cristofari	*Zoya's Story: An Afghan Woman's Struggle for Freedom.* New York: HarperCollins, 2003.
Norman Friedman	*Terrorism, Afghanistan, and America's New Way of War.* Annapolis, MD: Naval Institute Press, 2003.
Kathy Gannon	*I Is for Infidel: From Holy War to Holy Terror: 18 Years Inside Afghanistan.* New York: Public Affairs, 2005.
Larry P. Goodson	*Afghanistan's Endless War: State Failure, Regional Politics, and the Rise of the Taliban.* Seattle: University of Washington Press, 2001.
Michael Griffin	*Reaping the Whirlwind: Afghanistan, Al Qa'ida and the Holy War.* London: Pluto, 2003.
Victor Davis Hanson	*Between War and Peace: Lessons from Afghanistan to Iraq.* New York: Random House, 2004.
Rizwan Hussain	*Pakistan and the Emergence of Islamic Militancy in Afghanistan.* London: Ashgate, 2005.
Chris Johnson and Jolyon Leslie	*Afghanistan: The Mirage of Peace.* London: Zed, 2005.
Ann Jones	*Kabul in Winter: Life Without Peace in Afghanistan.* New York: Metropolitan, 2006.

Alexander Klaits, Gulchin Gulmamadova-Klaits
Love and War in Afghanistan. New York: Seven Stories, 2005.

Sean M. Maloney
Enduring the Freedom: A Rogue Historian in Afghanistan. Dulles, VA: Potomac, 2005.

Angelo Rasanayagam
Afghanistan: A Modern History. London: Tauris, 2003.

Ahmed Rashid
Taliban: *Militant Islam, Oil and Fundamentalism in Central Asia.* New Haven, CT: Yale Nota Bene, Yale University Press, 2001.

Jeffery J. Roberts
The Origins of Conflict in Afghanistan. Westport, CT: Praeger, 2003.

Barnett R. Rubin
The Fragmentation of Afghanistan: State Formation and Collapse in the International System. New Haven, CT: Yale University Press, 2002.

Amin Saikal
Modern Afghanistan: A History of Struggle and Survival. London: Tauris, 2004.

Gary Schroen
First In: An Insider's Account of How the CIA Spearheaded the War on Terror in Afghanistan. Novato, CA: Presidio, 2005.

Stephen Tanner
Afghanistan: A Military History from Alexander the Great to the Fall of the Taliban. Cambridge, MA: Da Capo, 2002.

Ana Tortajada   *The Silenced Cry: One Woman's Diary of a Journey to Afghanistan.* New York: Thomas Dunne, 2004.

Kim Whitehead   *Afghanistan: The Growth and Influence of Islam: In the Nations of Asia and Central Asia.* Broomall, PA: Mason Crest, 2005.

Batya Swift Yasgur   *Behind the Burqa: Our Life in Afghanistan and How We Escaped to Freedom.* Hoboken, NJ: Wiley & Sons, 2002.

Index